Adventures in C
True Stories of a Game Warden

Three decades of true stories and
a glimpse into what it's like to be a
Conservation Ranger.

Jim Hethcox

TO "Mr. Dick"
From "Miz Dick"
A GreaT Spor[t]
Jim

WP
PUBLISHING, INC
Metter, Georgia
2003

ADVENTURES IN GREEN AND GRAY

Published by Wiregrass Publishing, Inc.
Route 1 Box 220
Metter, Georgia 30439

Library of Congress Catalog Card Number: 2003110787
International Standard Book Number: 0-9743579-0-1

This book is a compilation of short stories by the author, based on true events throughout his career with the Georgia Department of Natural Resources, Game & Fish Division (later the Wildlife Resources Division), Law Enforcement Section. The names of persons involved in the stories have been changed, except for the author's name, department heads, or elected officials, to protect the identity of persons who may or may not wish to be identified in this publication. The author is aware that his experiences are not necessarily indicative of the career experiences of other wildlife officers but offers them as a sampling of his own account of nearly three decades of service to the people of the state of Georgia.

Printed in the United States of America

Cover Design by Rebecca Seel

- Table of Contents-

- Acknowledgments -

Since this book is based on my career as a Conservation Ranger, I feel that I must acknowledge those who have shaped my career. Without the career, there wouldn't be a book, so my acknowledgments should go to those who have been instrumental not only in the production of the book but also in the shaping of my career.

Throughout our lives we make decisions and take actions that set the direction and course of our existence on this earth. Some think that our actions are haphazard in nature but I have found them to be the Providence of God in action. At the time, I thought they were my decisions alone, only to discover years down the road that the course of my life was determined not by my actions but by the hand of God. Events are the products and not the cause of our determinations. In other words, our lives are ours, but they are steered by a higher power. Looking back, I can see a clear picture of what the grand design of my life was from the beginning.

One of the turning points in my life was the day I was hired as a Ranger. It fulfilled a desire I had since childhood. Little did I know to what extent the grand hand of design was employed in my affairs. So, I acknowledge the presence and plan of Almighty God in the events that have collectively become my life.

To Janice, I am eternally indebted for always being there and standing beside me no matter what was asked of her. She has been my inspiration, my partner, my life-long mate, and the dearest friend I've ever had. It was she who kept me going when things got tough. She alone came to my aid during the low points of my life with her kindness and understanding. She has been my helper and the department's unpaid employee through the years. Everybody needs someone in whom they can confide, and Janice has been my confidant.

It is with grateful appreciation that I render special thanks to my dear friend and kinsman, Hugh Richardson, who has graciously served as editor and advisor throughout this entire project. He has labored over the manuscript, correcting my many mistakes and forging it into a readable piece of work. His years of experience with the United States Air Force as editor of Airpower Journal have proven to be of great value to this work. The many hours he spent editing and correcting the manuscript and all the e-mails he sent and received to discuss the work are much appreciated. His kindness and sensitivity were the traits that have made him so easy to work with. He is demanding in excellence but not in temperance. His insistence on accuracy in every detail has transformed this manuscript into an enjoyable and easy read. I shall always be indebted to him for his kindness, patience, and hard work.

To my dear mother, I acknowledge with a grateful heart all the encouragement she has given me not only on this project but also throughout the years. It was she who urged me to apply with the Game & Fish, even when I didn't think I was qualified. It was she who went to great lengths to see that I got a fair consideration in the hiring process. It was she who checked on my status as the hiring process moved along, and it was she who discovered that I had been inadvertently dropped from the hiring list. If she hadn't been persistent, I would not have become a Ranger. I am convinced that God used her tenacity to bring about His plan for me. She has inspired me all my life and continues today to encourage and inspire. With a mother like her, I was obliged to excel.

Sergeant Irving G. Knox, Sr.

- Dedication -

First, I dedicate this book to my grandchildren, whose urging and insistence inspired me to pen my stories for their enjoyment long after I have departed from this scene. Their frequent request, "Papa, tell us another game warden story," was the driving force behind this book. I have endeavored to place in this book as many interesting happenings as I could put in print. Many of the things that happened during my career cannot be told in this publication. I have tried to keep this book clean in content. With the exception of an occasional quote I have succeeded in that charge.

Secondly, I dedicate this book to the memory of my first field sergeant, Irving G. Knox, Sr., whose training and advice have inspired me through the years. His words of advice and caution have kept me focused. There is a verse in the Bible that reminds me of Knox's influence on me. It is found in Hebrews 11:4 and reads, "He being dead yet speaketh." His philosophies of life and fatherly advice have inspired me throughout my career. His dry sense of humor added character to his personality. He was one of a kind and will be remembered as a good friend and dedicated associate.

- Chapter 1 -
Introduction

Georgia, the Empire State of the South, is the largest state east of the Mississippi River and one of the most diverse states in the country. She has mountains, rolling hills, coastal plains, swamps, rivers, lakes, trout streams, and the resource-rich Atlantic coastal waters. There is an abundance of wildlife resources in the state of Georgia. The state motto "Wisdom, Justice and Moderation" guides the leadership of Georgia in wisely managing this rich bounty while providing its citizens and guests with a multitude of opportunities to enjoy our great outdoors.

For years now I have taught our youngsters that our natural resources are a renewable resource and must be managed wisely. That is what conservation is all about. We have more wildlife numbers now than we did when Christopher Columbus discovered the new world. There are more deer, turkey, and many other species than there have ever been. This is due to carefully planned and executed management and protection plans and dedicated professionals who care about the resource.

I must also say that there are several species of wildlife that used to be very prolific in Georgia that do not exist anymore except in museum collections; mounted carcasses collecting dust and standing as a mute testimony that they once thrived in this land. Extinction is inevitable but nevertheless, sad to witness. Such species as the passenger pigeon, the Carolina parakeet, and the ivory-billed woodpecker once were bountiful, but they are now only memories and sketches in John James Audubon's books. I believe in conservation and have dedicated my life to its tenets.

That's where my story is born. For almost thirty years, I have been guided by these principles and was one of the ambassadors of conservation for the Georgia Department of Natural Resources. Ever since I was a little tyke I have always wanted to be a "Game Warden." This book is about some of the day-to-day experiences and adventures of that job. And yet, it's more than a job; it's a dedication, a career, a passion, and a way of life. To be a Conservation Ranger takes a special kind of person. One must be self-motivated and eager to go and keep going to accomplish the goals of good wildlife enforcement. You have to be able to work very odd hours and such varied days and hours that it is impossible to get into a set schedule. If a Ranger does that, he or she is not doing the job. That's all there is to it.

You may be up and out at 4:00 A.M. one morning checking baited stands or getting set up on a duck shoot or turkey blind long before the shooters show up. Then, you may have to work late evenings or even way past midnight to catch night deer hunters. There are those unforeseen circumstances that come along totally unannounced and always at the most inopportune times. I'm talking about things like a missing person report that may range from a two-year-old who wandered away to a nursing home patient with Alzheimer's who just walked out the door and is missing. These incidents always seem to happen in the winter when the temperature is predicted to drop down into the 20s or 30s during the night and you know that person won't make it unless you find them. All your personal plans, family plans, work plans, and any other schedules have to be put on hold while you literally try to snatch a victim from the hands of death.

Hunting accidents, boating accidents, and drownings are all a part of the Ranger's workload that happens when least expected or at least when something else is going on. Sometimes you have to drop everything and get into your vehicle or boat and go 10-18, blue lights and siren, to the scene of a tragedy. Once you get there you are the expert and control officer on the scene and you have to take charge and command and do what needs to be done immediately. Your training and preparation will help you to act instinctively to do what has to be done NOW! You have to be able to quickly sort the more important from the less important. You may have to protect a crime scene or keep traumatized family members away from a victim's body while you and/or others either administer life-saving first-responder measures or protect the body for the coroner and criminal investigation team.

Being a Ranger is one of the most admired and sought-after jobs in the public market. Many people would love to be a Ranger but know down in their hearts that they don't have what it takes to be one. Even though it is a much admired and sought-after job, it is also a thankless job. Many times Rangers do the work only to read in the newsprint where the sheriff's department or troopers get the credit for what they have done. I've even seen the Rangers get last billing behind the bloodhounds in a manhunt in which the Rangers actually caught the bad guy and had him handcuffed and turned over to the sheriff's deputies before the reporters got to the scene. Rangers know the backwoods, the back roads, the fields and streams, and most sheriffs who have any sense have learned to count on the Ranger to know the backwoods and be able to access the backcountry. Rangers usually are the only ones who have the four-wheel drive trucks, the all-terrain vehicles (ATVs), or boats, and can access where shiny shoes can't or won't go. One of my work partners used to tell people that the Conservation Rangers are the best-kept secret in state government. People didn't really know who I was or what I did. When they found out what I did, they were impressed. It is an impressive career and any young man or woman who goes for it should have what it takes and then try with all their might. It is really worth the trouble of wading through the hiring uniform and be one of Georgia's finest.

Rangers should not be surprised if people come in close to read their shoulder patch to figure out who they are and what they do. That's all part of being a member of the best-kept secret in state government. The few, the proud, the Green and Gray!

- Chapter 2-

What do you want to be when you grow up?

When I was about eight years old I remember contemplating what I wanted to be when I grew up. I remember thinking that I wanted to be a Marine and a fireman. That idea stuck with me most of my childhood until I reached my early teens. Then I began to take more interest in hunting and fishing. I remember my first .22 rifle. I was a terror on squirrels, and every chance I got during the squirrel season I would stay in the woods making the sport my main interest. We didn't have any deer in that part of the country where I was raised until later in the 1960s, so it was squirrels and rabbits that were my main pursuit. I would even build rabbit boxes and catch rabbits. I remember how my mother would fry those rabbits nice and crisp and then make some gravy and put the rabbit back into the gravy and let it simmer until it was just tender and tasty. She would make a big pan of hot biscuits, and boy was I in heaven.

Every once in a while I saw a local game warden drive by in his truck and that set my mind wondering what it would be like to be a game warden. Well, that idea soon overtook my earlier contemplations about being a fireman, and I found myself thinking more and more about being a game warden some day. I didn't know much about game wardens, but I knew that it had to be the best job in the world. I mean, what could be better than working at a career where you got to be outdoors all the time? My mind was made up. That's what I wanted more than anything in the world.

About the time I graduated from high school the draft was going strong because it was the mid 60s and Vietnam was going hot and heavy by then. As soon as I turned 18, I had to register with the local draft board and was sent almost immediately to Atlanta for my physical assessment and classification. Again, almost as soon as I had taken the physical, the mail brought the news that I was classified 1-A. They were drafting my high school buddies almost every day, so I knew that I would be called up just any day now.

My brother Steve and I and a buddy of ours, Robert Johnson, decided we would join the United States Marine Corps under the "Buddy System." We loaded up in Robert's old 57 Chevy and went to Atlanta to the Marine Corps recruiter's office. We had never heard so much talk about honor and esprit de corps, and before we knew it we were signed up. Talk about jumping out of the frying pan and into the fire! I guess I thought that I was in control of my own destiny. Besides, being a Marine was always in my plans. I've never regretted my time spent in the Marine Corps, and as long as I live I will always have that esprit de corps that my recruiter told us about. There is no such thing as an ex-Marine; it just seems to stay in your blood as long as you live.

After my military service was over, I returned to civilian life and got a job. But, the dream of being a game warden was never far from my mind. I guess I just thought that I wasn't good enough and almost gave up my dream. Then one day my mother, who worked for state government in Atlanta, encouraged me to put in my application and give it a try. After thirteen months of tests, physicals, physical agility testing, and just plain waiting for state government to work, it finally happened. On January 2, 1975, I began my first day at work as a Conservation Ranger for the Georgia Department of Natural Resources. I couldn't believe it! I was finally wearing the green and gray of Georgia's finest. The primary thought on my mind was that I had to do my best and make my family and my department proud of me. I guess that old Marine Corps pride of service has always been a driving force in my service to the state. Anyway,

I'm proud of my career as a Conservation Ranger and wouldn't take anything in the world for it. One of my friends who recently retired said at his retirement dinner that his career was like an eight-second bull ride at the rodeo. When the chute opened it was jam-packed with excitement, all the way to the buzzer. And I have also found that to be true. This past three plus decades have been a real joy for me personally and I have realized my lifelong dreams. What a blessed man I am for having been a Conservation Ranger.

I remember being interviewed by the colonel as a part of my pre-employment process. As I sat across the desk from him in his head-quarters office in Atlanta, I was in awe at his command appearance and demeanor. He was a no-nonsense type of guy and totally dedicated to the Game & Fish Division. In a feeble attempt to impress him I asked him that day if there was any such thing as a meritorious promotion in the Game & Fish. The Marine Corps had such a promotion for those who had shown themselves to be exemplary while in the field of service. His response to me was that all promotions in the Game & Fish were meritorious. Then, as I could feel myself melting into that seat from my embarrassment, he followed up with some advice that I have never forgotten. He said, "Ranger Hethcox, shoot for the moon, who knows, you just might miss and hit a star." With advice like that you can't help but do your level best always. I always tried not to disappoint that colonel during my career. And somewhere along the way I did just what he said, I did shoot for the moon and somehow I missed and hit a star. Fate, or rather God's providence, has a marvelous way of surprising us with something greater than we could have ever dreamed possible.

I have served under the leadership of three commissioners, three directors, seven colonels, six captains, and three field sergeants. All these men have helped to mold me as I made my way through my career. Their advice and personal training have molded me into what this new breed of Rangers respectfully call "the old corps," a title of which I am proud because it takes years of dedication to earn that title and not just length of years.

Realizing early on that being a successful Ranger is much more than catching bad guys and writing tickets, I began to put much emphasis on educating the public as to what we do and why. If you can win the hearts and minds of the public, they will support your operations and feel like they are a vital part of the big picture. There is no secret here. You have to be driven to write weekly newspaper articles, appear on television programs and radio talk shows, and even record a weekly radio spot highlighting local game and fish-related topics that the sportsmen and women find interesting. People will see you as a true public servant instead of that old SOB that is ruining their fun. Even the bad guys will gain respect for you. Information and education must be used in conjunction with strict enforcement if the whole program is to thrive. I have always tried to make new Rangers see this and maybe in some way help form them into what I call a well-rounded Ranger. In the long run it really pays off for the whole department.

As I progressed through my career I began to have a desire to pass along what I had learned to others. There aren't many Rangers and Technicians in Georgia that have not been in one of my training classes at one time or another. For years I have been involved with the Rangers' training academy. I helped train the first Ranger School at the old Georgia Police Academy on East Confederate Avenue in Atlanta. Later, we moved our training program to the new Georgia Public Safety Training Center facility in Forsyth. I have written lesson plans and taught such courses as History and Philosophy of Law Enforcement, The Ranger and the Public, Game

& Fish Laws, Courtroom Testimony & Demeanor, All Terrain Vehicle (ATV) Safety Training, Crime Scene & Evidence Photography, and last but not least, Emergency Vehicle Operator's Course (EVOC). That last one brought me the most enjoyment and feeling of accomplishment. I taught Rangers and Technicians how to handle an emergency vehicle in a high-speed chase or respond to an emergency call safely. I had the honor of being one of the pioneers in advancing this course in the Ranger School curriculum, which is still a major part of a new Ranger's training.

When I was a newly hired Ranger I set a goal of someday being a sergeant. It seemed to me to be the prime position in the agency. As it turns out, the position of sergeant is one of the agency's most important positions. I made sergeant in exactly four years from my hire date and stayed in that rank all the rest of my career. At the time of my retirement I was the senior sergeant in the state of Georgia. And, thinking back, it was like that eight-second bull ride--jam-packed excitement from start to finish. Thirty-one years went by so fast, and then it was over. I am left with my friends and my memories, many wonderful memories.

My first field sergeant told me when I began my career, "There were violators here before you were hired and there will be violators after you are gone; just do your part while you are here and let the loose ends drag." I think I did my part while I was in the arena and now it's time to let some young energetic Rangers take the helm for a while.

Over the years I have been asked by more young people than I can remember, "How do you become a Ranger?" My advice to them has always been to go to college and major in criminal justice or wildlife management studies and get your degree before applying. That's the best way to spend that time between high school and age twenty-one. You have to be at least twenty-one to work in law en-forcement, so you might as well spend that time preparing yourself for the competition that is coming.

I am proud to say that one of my cousins has just been hired as a new Ranger. He will graduate with a BS degree in criminal justice soon and start his Ranger School training. I know the excitement he is experiencing now and I wish him and all those young Rangers the very best in their careers. To them all I would say, "Just do your part while you are here and some day you can pass the baton on to the next runner."

- Chapter 3 -
Short Stories About Knox

Many of my best stories come from my relationship with my first field sergeant. He was a Ranger from the old school who had a dry sense of humor. The boys in his section admired his wit. He was an older guy, and all the Rangers in his supervisory section were young Rangers, mostly in their twenties. His dry humor was sometimes hard to follow. I thought the world of him and still do. He has been passed away for a few years now, but I shall always remember him. We just affectionately called him Knox. He was a doozy, to say the least.

The Choo Choo

One of my fellow Rangers who worked in Knox's section told the story about when he was a new employee working with Knox one night in another county in the district. Neither of them knew the county very well, especially at night. They were helping on a night deer-hunting detail in another Ranger's county several miles south of their area. Ranger John said that Knox was driving the car that night, and when they backed into position he noticed a set of railroad tracks about 20 feet or so behind the car. The passenger side of the patrol car was in straight line of sight with the railroad tracks, but they made a curve just before they got to where the car was parked. Evidently, Knox didn't see the tracks and wasn't aware that they were anywhere close to a train track. Do you get the picture? The new man sees the train tracks but the sergeant is unaware of anything nearby having to do with trains. As far as he knows, they are way out in the boonies away from civilization.

John said that about 11 o'clock he saw the headlight of a train several miles down the track but didn't say anything. Finally Knox noticed the light, which appeared to be coming closer and closer to John's side of the car. A train light seems to weave from side to side as it travels down the track. John said he thought Knox saw the light and knew it was a train. But the truth was that Knox hadn't seen the tracks, and so he thought it was a night hunter and didn't want to appear to be alarmed with the new man with him. So he played it cool as the light got closer and closer and suddenly the ground began to vibrate and then HONNK! HONNNNNNK! The train passed behind their car at a high rate of speed. John said that Knox was watching the light and just as the train began to take the curve it honked its horn long and loud. Knox began to scream at the top of his voice and jerk violently as he held on tightly to the steering wheel of the car. He was in a total body spasm as he let out a death-curdling scream. He thought he was about to die!

As the train's engine passed behind the patrol car, the boxcars rumbled past in the cold night, vibrating and rumbling the earth. The train finally passed and moved on out of sight and hearing.

When everything returned to quiet and peacefulness, John said he didn't say a word for fear he would die laughing at the sergeant and get into trouble. Then, calmly the sergeant asked, "John, did you see that train track when we got into position tonight?" "Yes, Sergeant," John replied. "Well, why in blazes didn't you say some-thing about it?" asked Knox. At that, John couldn't hold it any longer and busted out laughing at Sergeant Knox. When he finally got to where he could control himself, Knox told him that he'd better not tell anybody about this or John wouldn't make permanent status. It was a long time before John told that story, but it's a good one and Knox even laughed at it later.

Quail Hunting

Then there was the time when Knox caught a man hunting quail illegally. Instead of paying his fine, the man, who apparently wanted to protect his reputation as a hot shot, took the case to court and hired a lawyer to get him off this charge. I think it was a source of embarrassment to this man more than the guilt. He wanted to make Knox look bad in court and get his case thrown out of court.

Knox said the defense attorney had him on the witness stand and asked him several questions trying to find a weakness in his story. He asked Knox how he knew the man was hunting, and Knox told him that he had a bird dog and was walking around in quail habitat with a shotgun in his hands looking for quail. Then, the defense attorney thought he had him where he wanted him and asked Knox sarcastically, "Well, Sergeant, if I was walking around in the open field with a shotgun, looking up in the sky, would you say that I was hunting airplanes?" "Well, sir," Knox said slowly, "if you had three in your sack I would!" At that, the courtroom burst out in laughter, and the attorney convinced his client to give up and ask for mercy. His client was found guilty and had to pay a fine and a lawyer's fee. Knox's reputation grew in that part of the country because of that case.

How Far Can You See At Night?

Then there was the time when Knox had caught a man hunting deer at night. This man, too, was trying to get a lawyer and get out of the charge. With Knox on the stand, the attorney commanded him to "Tell the court what you saw that night." "Well, sir, I saw this man shoot at a deer from about two hundred yards away, so I made the case against him," said Knox. "Well now, Sergeant, would you mind telling the court just how far you can see at night?" quipped the attorney. "I can see the moon, how far is that?" asked Knox.

Get 'em up!

One day Knox was working with me on Clarks Hill Lake. That is one thing that Knox didn't do much. He didn't like working on the lake. He said that was for us young boys to do so he stayed out of the boating safety work. He would ride the hill and transport drunks and prisoners to jail for us, but he usually didn't get into the boat. But there was this one day when he decided he would run the boat and show me how they "used to do it in the old days." One of our usual methods of checking life preservers on a boat where there were several people was to get each person to hold up a life preserver.

Knox was driving our boat and we came alongside a boat full of people who were having a good time on the lake. He pulled our boat directly toward their boat at a pretty high rate of speed and turned it just in time to avoid us hitting them. I just knew we would hit their boat, but we just glided right alongside them as if he had planned it that way. Until today I still don't know if that was experience or blind luck at work. Anyway, as we came to a halt he demanded the occupants to "Get 'em up!" He, of course, meant for each person to hold up a life preserver, but they didn't understand it that way. All of a sudden everybody on board held their hands up in the air in a surrender mode with eyes wide open as if they were in a holdup. Those poor folks didn't know Knox or how he operated, and it took some smoothing over to get them calmed down. They thought there was a law enforcement emergency and they were somehow suspects in some unknown crime. I was too busy playing the casual cop to be embarrassed. I remember being glad when that day was over.

Too Many Jims

On the first day of my employment, I reported to the district office to meet the captain and field sergeant and get my initial issue. After a few hours of first-day orientation, the captain called my sergeant into the office to meet me. It was my first meeting with Knox. When he arrived, I was quite struck at his stature. He was a fairly short man with a distinct Scottish look about him and a twinkle in his eye that reminded me of the Irishman, Darby O'Gill, in the Walt Disney movie, "Darby O'Gill and the Little People." When the captain introduced me to him, he told Knox that my name was Jim. Well, Knox just looked at me and said, "No it ain't." "Excuse me?" I asked. "I don't know what your name is yet, but it ain't Jim; we got too many Jims around here already," Knox said. I didn't have a clue as to what he meant, and I thought he was quite out of line telling me what my name was not!

Come to find out, there were already four Jims in the district and I would make the fifth. So Knox thought that he would give me another name. He never, as long as he lived, called me Jim. But about a month later, he came by to pick me up and asked me, "Hey, Jeff, do you want to go on patrol with me?" "What did you call me, Sarge?" I asked. "From now on your name is going to be Jeff," he said. And that was that! He had a knack of making a nickname stick, and it stuck so well that my own wife even began calling me Jeff. She would leave me a note on the table or fridge saying, "Dear Jeff, I've gone to the grocery store. Be back in a little while." It really stuck through the years and people all over the state called me Jeff right up until the time I retired. And I had Knox to thank for that. As a matter of fact, when my wife was pregnant with our third child I had already decided that if it was a boy I wanted to name it Jeff so I could get my name back, but she was a girl. It seemed that I was destined to be stuck with the nickname of Jeff.

Knox is Gone

At the time Knox died, I was living and working in another part of the state and hadn't seen him in a long time. I would call him on the phone from time to time. He had lost much of his hearing and wouldn't talk on the phone except when "Jeff" called. I believe he loved me like a son, and I have to say I loved him like a father. His own three sons are fine men and well thought of in their community. His widow loved me and still does today. Knox's reputation of being one of the best game wardens in the state still lives in the east-central section of Georgia. When he died, we laid a legend to rest. So long, old soldier, we will meet again.

- Chapter 4 -
The Night of Death

It was December 1978. Weather-wise it had been a strange day. Earlier that day I was working around my new house near Harlem. We had just had it built about five months earlier and there was a lot of yard work to be done. It had been an unusually busy fall and winter, and my time at home had been extremely limited. I remember the weather that day was in the low 70s but sunny and breezy and I had been working in short sleeves in the yard. I had planned to do some night work so I was taking my time off early in the day. For a winter day, it was unusually balmy, and I remember thinking how nice it was to be able to get an advance on the spring.

The rest of the upper part of the district had planned a night flight in the lower part of the district, and I was not included in their plans because I had been having some trouble with night hunters on the Baker Place Road and wanted to work on that. My field sergeant told me to go ahead and work that alone because everybody else would be down south that night.

As the day passed, a strong frontal system was moving in and the temperature really dropped fast. The forecast was that it would be in the low 20s before morning and we were in for some cold and windy weather. That's what I meant about it being a strange day weather-wise. It was spring-like in the morning and arctic-like at night.

There was a major reservoir in my county and I knew the chance was always there that someone would need help on the lake at any time. Winter was not a fit time to be on the lake and few got on the water, especially on such a windy and deteriorating day. The lake was unusually low because we were in a drought and most of the boat ramps on the lake were above the waterline and therefore unusable. I kept my boat in a boathouse on the state park. The boat-house was anchored over a really deep rock-bottom cove and there-fore there was always enough water there. That being the case, I left my boat in the boathouse during the winter months just in case somebody needed a rescue or in case of a drowning. All the other Rangers had taken their boats out of the water and winterized them. Mine was the only boat on the lake that was in the water and usable in a moment's notice.

My boat was an older model seventeen-foot patrol boat with a six-cylinder Chevrolet engine in it. It had a blue light on the bow that was huge and one of those old mechanical sirens that would wind up and whine forever if you ever hit the switch. It was a real antique, but we were in tight times budget-wise and the captain could do no better for now. I had just done some deck repairs on her and had her in the shop for some much needed repairs to make her seawor-thy in case she was needed during the winter.

My wife had made me a big thermos of coffee and some sand-wiches, and I was ready to go to my secret spot on the Baker Place Road when I got a call from the sheriff's office. The dispatcher told me that he had just received a call from a sailboat skipper on the lake who had run aground on an island and was stranded. The boater's report was that he was wet, tired, and cold and needed somebody to come rescue him off that island. I grabbed my thermos and goodies, and as I went out the door I asked my wife to call my sergeant and tell him of my change in plans and what I would be doing. As she headed toward the phone, I rushed out the door. The Baker Place Road night hunters would have to wait for another night to go to jail. There was a man on the lake in big trouble. I knew that if that boater was wet and cold he would die of hypothermia before morning and he needed somebody now. It was truly a life and death response.

With that cold front rushing in, the lake was as rough as I had ever seen it. It definitely wasn't a night to be on the lake. It wasn't so bad in the protected cove where my boathouse was, but as I went out toward the Little River run of the lake, things got serious really fast. The waves were at least six feet high and there was a gale-force wind coming out of the west. Luckily, the waves were going in my direction so I didn't have to fight against them. I'll have to admit, I was more scared than I had ever been on that lake. It was nothing like the warm, sunny weather that usually accompanied boat operation. This was a very serious situation and the worst I'd ever been in. I was beginning to wish I had somebody with me to help with the rescue when I reached the sailboat. It would be really tough by myself but I had no choice. I had to get there and fast! I wondered about the stranded boater and what he must be feeling about now. It truly was a howling night, and you could just feel something ominous in the air.

Heck, by now I was feeling really small in a big, dark, storm-tossed lake. I was headed toward the Little River Bridge and I knew that once I went under the bridge I could go behind the roadway's riprap and be somewhat better protected from the wind and waves. That was my plan for the moment. I had to get through the bridge and then break right, behind the shelter of the built-up roadway. It was one of those long highway bridges where the roadway was built up by large granite rocks to bring the road out to meet the bridge. It was just perfect to break the waves up. Everything would be better beyond the Little River Bridge.

But as I fought the waves and slowly steered toward the bridge, the boat engine just shut off. I was still about a half a mile from the bridge and now my boat shut off. I tried over and over to crank it, but it wouldn't even hit a lick. It was almost like the engine wasn't getting fire. I removed the cowling from the engine and everything had been drenched by the waves coming over into my boat. The bilge pump was spurting water as fast as it could, and here I was drifting with the storm of the century. I knew my battery wouldn't take the constant spinning and the bilge pump so I began to think of what to do. I had to use my radio before my battery went down. If I didn't, no one would know my plight.

The local state patrol office in Thomson had a game and fish radio in their radio room. I wondered if they would have it turned on or if the volume would be turned down too low to hear. That radio operator would be my only hope. I called, "352 to GSP Thomson, can you copy me?" No answer! Holy Cow! I had to try again. "352 to Thomson, do you copy?" After about the third try I was wondering if the battery had already gone out and then I heard, "Thomson to 352, go ahead." Man, was I ever glad to hear that voice. I began to tell the operator that I was adrift in the Little River run of the lake and that I was on my way to rescue a sailboat operator on that island. I asked him to call the Columbia County Rescue Squad to handle the sailboat's call and send someone to the Little River Bridge to pick me up. I really didn't think the Rescue Squad could launch a boat but I had no choice. Now I was in trouble. I saw that I was not going to drift through the bridge's opening. I was going to be thrashed into those huge granite rocks supporting the highway. I told the radio operator of my situation and signed off.

Once again I tried to crank her, but by now the battery was really low. It was useless. I had to come up with a plan now to try to save my own hide. I have never in my life felt like I did that cold stormy night. I could feel the chilling shroud of death around me and for the first time in my young life I really thought it might end there that night.

As I got closer and closer to the riprap I began to hear and see the waves crashing against the big rocks of the roadway. It looked like the California west coast in a storm. Wow! I had never seen anything like that on Clarks Hill Lake. It looked like waves crashing on an ocean, not on an inland lake. Up until now the worst I had seen on that lake was just some white capping, but this … this was different for sure! The waves would lift my boat several feet into the air and then drop me like a hot potato, just to do it all over again and again and again. As I watched the timing of the waves I got a plan. Just before I hit the rocks, the last act I did from my boat was to throw my thermos as far up toward the highway guardrail as I could throw it. I knew if I lived through this I would need something warm. The thermos was of stainless steel, and I knew it wouldn't break. That thing was nearly as big as a propane bottle but I gave it a sling and then I went up carefully onto the bow of the boat. I rolled up the bowline and held it in my left hand while I held on to that big siren with my right hand. There I was, perched on the bow holding the rope and that big bow-mounted siren. I'd have given a million bucks for a good anchor about ten minutes earlier.

What I planned to do was to jump onto the rocks just as the wave lifted my boat high and close. It had to be the lift of the last wave prior to hitting the rocks. Timing and speed were everything. I would jump onto the rocks at the height of the wave's lift and try to pull the bowline around a big rock. I really hoped to tie the boat off high into the rocks before it dropped back into the depths. Now, admittedly, that was a lot to do in a short time. Think about it-- jump onto the rocks, catch my own footing, lash the bowline around a big rock, and hope the boat wouldn't thrash around on those rocks too much until the storm passed. Yep. You're right. It wasn't much of a plan, but it was all I had and it didn't work out the way I had hoped. There was just too much to do in too short a time. Here's what happened. I timed it right and made my jump. But about the time I was trying to catch my footing the boat had already dropped to the lowest point of the wave and it viciously snatched the rope out of my hand. It gave me a strong snatch and I began to fall beneath the boat in the darkness below. I began to scamper up the rocks with a new zeal. It was time to move and move fast. It was live or die time and I knew it.

I really wanted to save the boat, but now I knew that my first concern had to be to save my own life. My greatest fear had now been realized. I had been dragged down the slippery rocks by the wave action and was about to be crushed by the boat with the next wave. I was really scared and I don't mind admitting that. It was past time to pucker and I was doing some heavy-duty puckering for sure. With lightning speed, I scampered up those rocks just before the boat fell on the rocks where I had been. After I caught my breath, I could see that the boat had already taken on a lot of water and was partially sunk. It wasn't thrashing about as violently as before, so I climbed down the rocks and found the bowline again. I tied her off as high up into the rocks as I could and began a damage assess-ment. It looked like the hull was split down the side like a pecan shell and the heavy engine was resting on the rocks. She wouldn't be damaged any more than she already was. My first thought was what would the captain say about me losing one of the state's boats. I wondered if he would be angry with me for the loss of the vessel or be thankful that he didn't lose a Ranger that terrible night. Oh well, I'd worry about that later. Now I had to think about trying to keep warm and keep from getting hypothermia.

Cars came down the highway and I tried to wave them down, but no one would stop. I wondered if the state patrol had gotten in touch with anybody. I knew all the Rangers had gone down south for the night flight. As it turned out, the flight was cancelled because of the weather, but they worked the detail anyway. I hoped the state patrol would call the sheriff's department and have a deputy pick me up. I was cold and wet and couldn't stand on that windy road all night, so I began to walk. After several minutes, a truck came up to me and stopped. It was the park superintendent who had been called to pick me up. Boy, was I happy to see him! As I stepped into the warm truck, I told him the story and asked him to go back to the boat with me. I thought of some things that I would need to get out of the boat before I left it for the night.

He then took me around to my vehicle at the boathouse, and as I started the car up and turned the radio on I could hear the sheriff's department dispatcher talking to the rescue squad members, and I went to the sheriff's department. Upon arrival, I was told that two men and a little boy were missing on the lake. The rescue squad had been able to launch a boat, and they had picked up the stranded sailboat skipper. For that I was thankful. At least he and I would live through this night. I was thanking God for saving me that night. For a while there it had been close.

I learned the next day that two men, brothers, and the little boy of one of them had been out fishing in a small boat the day before. The pretty weather early in the day fooled them. They had been on an island and darkness had caught them before they could return to shore. They had tried to maneuver that little open boat through those raging waves, but their boat was soon capsized. All three managed to hold on to the overturned boat in the rough seas. The water was very cold, and they knew they were in trouble. One of the brothers told the other one that he was going to try to swim for the shore even though they couldn't see the shore. He didn't know which direction to swim, but he took off anyway and was not seen again.

He drowned that night, and it was several months before his body was located. I have never seen a body stay down that long. It was believed that his body was caught on some structure and didn't float as it normally would. Some people even thought that he had been caught in the gates of the dam intake. It was a really bad situation.

The other brother, the father of the little boy, had tied a life preserver around his son. The water and waves were just too rough for him to get it on him properly and he could only manage to get it tied to him. Yes, I agree, the little boy should have been wearing it all along anyway, but people will do some foolish things.

After a long while, the man told us that he was later holding the overturned boat by the bow while holding his son and eventually realized that his son was dead. He had died from hypothermia. The storm had claimed the second victim of the night. The father, then out of his head with grief and cold, decided to try to swim for it too. He pushed off just like his brother had done earlier and began to swim away into the cold darkness of this night of death.

His story was that he swam and swam until he finally decided that he just didn't have enough strength to keep trying. He decided to give up and just drown. Totally exhausted, he stopped swimming and began to go down. He said that he felt his feet hit the bottom and realized that he was not in deep water now. That gave him new hope and a burst of adrenaline, so he kicked to the surface and tried to swim again. He saw car lights a little way off and, mustering all the strength he could, he swam toward the roadway. He said he finally got to where he could just barely tiptoe on the bottom. Then, at last, he made his way to the road. After managing to pull himself up to the roadway, he was picked up by a passing motorist and taken to a hospital. By a miracle of God and his own will to survive, he lived through that terrible night of death. However, his brother and his son were victims of that freak winter storm. What mixed emotions and feelings he must have had in the days that followed.

Oh, by the way, the captain ordered us to take the boat to the shop so they could determine what made it stop running that night. After flushing the water out of it, the mechanic tried to crank it and it wouldn't fire. Then he discovered that the coil had shorted out. It was something that couldn't have been prevented or known beforehand. It was just one of those things that caused a big "if" in my life. I have wondered what if my boat hadn't stalled that night, could I maybe have come across the small overturned boat with the two men and little boy holding on? Could I have saved them from certain death just by coming by and pulling them aboard? What if, what if, what if?

Over the years I have remembered the feeling I had that night when it felt like a death shroud was around me. I didn't know it at the time, but death was taking its prey on Clarks Hill Lake on that cold December night. I just thank God that he spared me to come home to my family that night.

- Chapter 5 -
Monkey Business

For the most part, Rangers are accustomed to encountering and handling wildlife that is indigenous to the state where the rangers are assigned. Occasionally, however, there appears the "problem" animal that has to be handled.

Monkey Story 1

Such was the case once when I was instructed by my captain to meet a certain man and pick up his bear and monkey and help him transport them to a nearby zoo where they had appropriate facilities for handling such wild animals. The bear was reported to me as being a Himalayan Sun Bear and the monkey was, well, who knows what! The man, who was an Atlanta policeman, was holding the animals without proper permits. The man had a nice family that ran a local restaurant where the Rangers often ate, so the captain didn't want to charge him with a violation but did want the problem removed and the family to come into compliance with the laws. So, on the appointed date, I met with the man who already had the bear enclosed in a bear trap. This bear had been kept at one of the department's fish hatchery facilities where they had built a wildlife zoo for school children to visit on their field trips to see the wildlife. Now the bear had become somewhat difficult after repeatedly breaking out of his pen.

The bear had recently escaped, and one of the fisheries technicians had tried to lure the bear back to the pen with a jar of honey. When he had led the bear to the pen entrance, the man pitched the honey into the pen, but it didn't go far enough, so the bear was only half way in when the technician put his foot against the bear's behind and gave it a big push. Well, now, Mr. Bear didn't like that at all so he turned and mauled the man pretty badly. He was hospitalized for a week or so, but it was plain by then that the bear had to go.

Needless to say, I was very concerned about this bear, but we loaded the bear-trap (with bear) into the back of my pickup truck and closed the tailgate. All's well so far. Now, he had put that monkey into the cab inside a cardboard box and had closed the top with a fold, and a fold, and a fold, and a tuck, which left a small opening in the top of the box. The monkey kept trying to push his head through the box opening. This was not a good situation, but we headed down the road late in the afternoon just before dark.

All the way down the road, that monkey kept trying to get out of that box and the guy in the cab with me would slap the monkey's head back into the box with a gloved hand. After being slapped several times in the face, the monkey finally got smart. Yep, you guessed it! When the man slapped at him the next time, the monkey was ready and bit through the glove. He nailed that guy really good through the finger with those nasty, needle-sharp teeth. Well, you can guess what the man's reflexes caused him to do. He jerked his hand back and along with it came the attached monkey. When that varmint got loose in the cab of my truck, he went crazy. He ran around that truck so fast you could hardly see him and all the time he was crapping all over the place. He was running from the windshield over my shoulder and head to the back window around and around inside that truck. All the time he was doing this, he was screaming loudly with the shrillest pitch you can imagine, and the adrenaline of three of God's creatures was exploding. Now, picture this: We're traveling about 60 miles per hour after dark on a four-lane highway in going-home traffic in Augusta, Georgia, in the drizzling rain; the monkey is screaming, I'm screaming, and the guy is screaming, and all the time I am jamming on the brakes and hitting the ditch as fast and hard as I possibly could.

As soon as the truck came to a stop--well, actually it was just before the truck came to a stop-- we exited the truck and left the doors open. That monkey just sat on the seat looking at me as if he wanted me to hand him the gas card so he could go on his merry way. While I kept the monkey's attention, the man nabbed him in the back of the neck with a gloved hand and held him in his lap. All the time, the man was screaming, "Shut my door and let's get the heck out of here!" I ran around and slammed his door, jumped back in the truck and proceeded with blue lights and siren to the zoo, which was only a few miles away, while this guy held on to that blasted monkey with all his might. Now remember, there is a mean-spirited bear in the back, and to be honest with you, I hadn't given him a second thought. After all, I was armed and dangerous as far as he was concerned, and I was taking no prisoners tonight!

After we delivered the animals to the little privately owned zoo in Hephzibah, we went to a car wash and spent several quarters trying to get the monkey crap out of the truck and off us. What a night! Thinking back, as I pondered what it would be like to be a Ranger, I never in my wildest dreams thought I'd be hauling a loose and crazed monkey in the cab of my truck. After that night, I never hauled any-thing that was not human in the front of my truck again. All other passengers must be caged and ride in the rear. Experience is al-ways the best teacher.

Monkey Story 2

There was another monkey that was kept at that same wildlife zoo, and I'm pretty sure this one was a Macaque. To say the least,

he was a really mean one. So many people had picked at him that
he just had the disposition of an old curmudgeon or someone with
an overdose of PMS. In short, he was like an incident looking for
something to happen all over. I don't know why, but it has always
seemed to me that monkeys are nasty-tempered animals and not
worthy of our affection. This particular Macaque was kept in a wire
pen that was elevated off the ground with concrete blocks for sanita-
tion purposes.

One day a visiting technician went to the monkey pen and had a
couple of pieces of bread in his hand to feed the nice monkey. As
the man approached the pen, the monkey kept a sharp eye on him.
He pitched the bread in the direction of the monkey, and the monkey
just let it fall through the pen floor without trying to catch it or even
look at it. He just ignored it altogether. Well, the man came around
to the corner of the pen where the monkey was and stooped down
and reached under the pen to retrieve the bread so he could make a
second attempt to be nice to the monkey. No such luck! As soon as
the man's head got up against the wire, the monkey lunged toward
the man with both hands open for a full two-handed grip on his head
hair. That mean monkey began to rattle the man's head against the
cage like he was ringing a bell. The man was yelling, and the monkey seemed to be grinning while he was having the time of his life
pulling that poor man's hair.

I think the man, who was already balding, lost a double handful
of what little hair he had left at the monkey pen that day. The monkey just climbed back onto his perch and looked contented as if he
knew he had just harassed a human being.

- Chapter 6 -
Ducking Across the Line

For several years I maintained my Deputy Federal Game Warden Commission. This unique office enabled me to enforce federal game violations in Georgia. The jurisdiction of the federal commission also covered all the states that share a border with Georgia. One of the benefits of such a commission was that of being able to cross the state line in the enforcement of the migratory bird and waterfowl laws. This came in handy to us who worked in a state line county. It meant that theoretically we could pursue a violator into an adjoining state. Only once in my entire career did the circumstances make it necessary to do just that. The United States Supreme Court has recognized that enforcement officers of one state can proceed into an adjoining state if in hot pursuit of an actual or suspected violator of the law.

Living in Columbia County, Georgia, made it really handy to have that federal commission. Since Columbia County was on the state line of South Carolina and the Fort Gordon military base was in much of the county, I found myself in many situations where my federal commission might come in handy.

One such situation occurred during the duck season one winter. As it turned out that particular day, the duck season was open in South Carolina but closed in Georgia. My partner and I were working the Savannah River to insure that no one decided to open the season in Georgia also. We had hidden our boat in some bulrushes in the water's edge on the Georgia side just north of the northern point of Tuning Fork Island. This island was all in Georgia, and the state line came just to the Carolina side of the northern point of the island and then went further toward the center of the river. We watched as late in the afternoon a boatload of men approached the marshy point of the island and began putting out decoys. After shooting hours in either state, the ducks began to come in and the slaughter began. These guys were banging away at the great hoards of ducks trying to land in the vicinity of their decoys. Just as it was getting too dark to see, they began collecting their ducks and decoys and promptly headed toward the South Carolina side of the river.

I cranked our 14-foot fiberglass boat with a 20-horsepower motor and proceeded toward the point from which they had left. The darkness obscured them, and we had to chase sound. What we had to do was chase the wake and bubbles until we couldn't detect them and then abruptly shut the engine off and give a quick listen. Once we regained our bearing, I gave the rope a quick jerk and off we went again in pursuit of our violators.

By now we were well within the boundary of the state of South Carolina and headed toward the eastern bank, but I kept going. Until this day I'm not sure if they knew they were being chased, because the sound of their engine drowned out our engine's noise. Then again, they just may have been out-powered. At any rate, we caught up to them just before they reached the Carolina bank. They looked back and saw us in the darkness and knew then that the game wardens were hot on their tails. The operator yelled something to the other two, and as soon as they hit the bank they ran toward the front of their boat and jumped out trying to climb the steep red clay bank. My partner was poised just like a jump dog on our bow and as soon as I came alongside, he sprang out and caught both those guys and pulled them back down the bank and into our waiting grasp. Man, was that exciting! It was three to two but we had them out-manned. I grabbed the boat operator and we announced that we were Rangers. "Y'all are Georgia boys, ain't you?" came the operator's question. At that, we took out our federal commission credentials and announced that we were enforcing the Federal Migratory Bird Act. In other words, we were arresting them for the federal offense of shooting after hours. We then began to check the plugs in their shotguns, their licenses, Federal Migratory Bird Stamps, and to count the ducks. They were badly over the daily bag limit even if they had been in South Carolina when they had shot them. We informed them that they were hunting illegally in Georgia waters at the time of their violations but we were putting the cases in the federal courts.

We wrote their citations out and advised them they would be notified by the federal prosecuting attorney's office as to when and where to appear. Most likely it would be in the Federal Court Building in Augusta, but that wasn't for us to say. We seized their ducks and left them on the Carolina bank as we proceeded back to the Empire State of the South, sweet Georgia land.

As soon as I got home that night, I called the federal agent that covered my area and told him what we had done and he set everything up for the court date. Although we had those jurisdictional concessions, we always had to run our federal cases by the federal agent in charge of our area. He was a good guy and a stern enforcement officer so he was strongly behind us.

When the court day arrived, my partner and I arrived a little early in the courtroom and the judge was already seated and quietly handling some paper shuffling. We just sat quietly waiting for the defendants to arrive.

When they came into the courtroom, the judge looked up and began to smile and chat with these guys as old friends. As it turned out, the judge and the defendants were good buddies. They were calling each other by first name and shaking hands and it looked like an old fraternity reunion. Holy cow! Can you believe it? Of all the people in the world, we had to catch the judge's buddies. Man, what a waste of time this was going to be!

Finally, after what seemed like an eternity, the judge called the court to order and after having us sworn in, we gave our testimony. The judge asked the defendants if this was true and they just said, "Yes, your honor." With that, the judge looked over his reading glasses and declared them all guilty on all charges. He then proceeded to dispense some of the strictest fines I had ever seen. Before they left the courtroom that day, their "good buddy" judge had cleaned them out, good buddies or not. I couldn't believe it! We had not only won our cases, but we had won the day. I shall never forget that federal judge. He taught us all a lesson that day. When it comes to business, he didn't play around, and neither did we.

- Chapter 7-
The Dumbull

Every once in a while a really good practical joke presents itself and everyone can have a good time with it. Such was the case of the Dumbull, known in some circles as a Whang-Doodle. Never heard of a Dumbull? Well, let me tell you what a Dumbull is. A Dumbull can be made from a large can or small bucket. You take the can and cut the top out of it. Then put a small hole in the bottom through which you run a rawhide bootlace or rope, soaked with kerosene. The kerosene gives it the right vibrating tension when you pull it. You tie a knot in the rawhide strap inside the can and let the loose end hang out the bottom of the can. By grabbing the rawhide at the base of the can and giving it a pull so as to let the strap slip through your finger and thumb, you can set up a vibration that will scare a body to death. That vibration resonates through the can and like a homemade speaker it gives a blood-curdling moan like a wooly booger or something. It really sounds spooky and will make the hair stand up on the back of your neck even though you know all the time what it is.

The real fun comes when you make that awful moaning for someone who doesn't know what it is. It sounds like Bigfoot or Sasquatch whooping out a mating call and can give an awful scare to an unsuspecting victim. You can even put your free hand over the opening of it and wave your hand giving it a "whaaa-ooo-whaaa-ooo-whaaa-oooooooooo" sound.

One day I was at the maintenance shop at the state park getting some gasoline in my state truck. A Park Ranger, who is a good friend of mine named Jerry, was down there fooling around with a Dumbull he had made. I had never seen one, and Jerry was giving me a demonstration and putting on quite a show with it. Like I said, that sound can give you the willies. That moaning sounded like the devil himself. And, friends, was it ever loud! We all had a good laugh and went about our business.

A couple of nights later, we had a church league softball game and Jerry and I were telling Ray, the pastor, about that Dumbull. As it turns out, Jerry was going to take a young fellow from the church on a camping trip at the state park that night after the ball game. They had planned to camp out in the Pioneer Camping Area on the state park, and had already set up their tent earlier that day. The young fellow's name was Clay, and he was an Army brat. Jerry was a real outdoors guy whom Clay thought the world of. Clay had never camped out, and Jerry was his hero. Clay was about fifteen or so and had his parents' permission to camp with Jerry. They were looking forward to Clay's first camp-out.

I really don't remember whose idea it was, but one of us came up with the idea of pulling a joke on Clay that night with the Dumbull. Our game plan went something like this. After the softball game, Jerry would take Clay to their camping area and build a fire. In the meantime, Ray and I would go to the maintenance shop and get that Dumbull and work our way down through the woods to the Pioneer Camping Area. There were no fancy facilities at the Pioneer Camping Area, just running water and an outdoor toilet. Yep, it was an old-fashioned "crescent-moon-in-the-door" outhouse.

Ray and I gave Jerry and Clay time to get in camp and build a fire while we made our way through the woods to the area. We saw their campfire flickering through the woods and made our way to within fifty yards or so of where they were camping. They were both sitting by the fire talking as I got set up with the Dumbull. I put the can in the bend of my knee and placed my free hand over the mouth of the can, pointed it in their direction and gave the string a pull. It made a low "grunt" sound. Just one or two at first was all it took to get their attention. Now, get this picture. Ray and I are outside the camp with ill intentions and Jerry is working on the fears of Clay from the inside. Jerry is our inside man and Clay is the unsuspecting victim. We were just playing this thing by ear, but it was beginning to look like we might have some fun tonight.

At first I started out with a few grunt sounds and then I began to work up to a short moan. All the time I worked the Dumbull, I could barely hear Jerry telling Clay that he had never, in all his days in the woods, heard anything like that. Clay asked him if he thought it might be a bear and Jerry told him no, that a bear didn't sound like that. He kept telling Clay that he didn't know what it was. Jerry was really doing his job. We were making a slow circumference of their camp while pulling on the Dumbull ever so often. We made Clay think this thing was circling their camp getting ready to attack. As we circled, we moved closer and closer until we got within a few feet of the back of their tent. By the time we got directly behind their tent we were making the Dumbull really stand up and moan. It was a most frightening sound in those dark Georgia woods that night.

We thought they had gone inside the tent because we could no longer see them anywhere. During our crawling and moving from spot to spot we had lost sight of them. I began to pitch small sticks and pine cones on the back of the tent but I could hear nothing from them. They had quit talking and I had, quite frankly, lost track of where they were.

I whispered really low to Ray, "Where did they go?" "I don't know," he whispered back. Then, we heard one of them whispering from inside the outhouse. Yes, they had gone inside the outhouse to get away from the unknown booger. It was a most appropriate place to scare the mess out of somebody. What a break! Ray and I moved right up to the back of the outhouse.

I began to grunt on the Dumbull while Ray leaned against the outhouse with his shoulder and made it rock a little. I made blowing sounds as if something big was sniffing the prey inside. This went on for a little while and then we heard Clay in a loud whisper ask Jerry, "What are we going to do?" To which Jerry said excitedly, with each word getting louder and faster, "I don't know about you, but I'm getting the heck out of here!" I had to move fast. I positioned myself just around the corner of the outhouse door and about that time the door almost came off the hinges as they both ran out, Jerry first and then Clay right on his heels. I let Jerry get past me, and when Clay burst out into the darkness, I grabbed him in the chest with both hands and at the same time made a growling roar with my voice as loud as I could. As I grabbed at him and growled, he cried out with a scream and lit out like his pants were on fire. This was the height of the whole night's doings. This was the moment when we tried to scare the heck out of him, and we almost did. That young fellow started running while we fell to the ground laughing.

Jerry, Ray, and I were laughing so hard we almost lost our breath. Clay was scared and mad at the same time, but he knew he had been "had" by his best friends. After he caught his breath he came back to where we were rolling on the ground in laughter, and had a good laugh with us. We really got him good that night. I think Clay will never forget his first camping trip with the compliments of his old buddies Jerry, Ray, me, and a very special new friend, the Dumbull. Clay told everybody that he knew about the Dumbull. He wanted to borrow it from Jerry and play the same joke on his little brother and his friends.

- Chapter 8-
I Ain't Got No License

There is a place on the Savannah River just above Augusta that's called the Old City Locks. It is a favorite fishing spot for local folks because you can fish in the river or in the canal. The fishing is usually good there and therefore it's a popular spot for Richmond and Columbia County citizens. At one time the state record striped bass had come from those waters. It was also one of my favorite spots for license checks as it usually proved to be a fruitful place for checking. You almost never saw the same people there, as it seemed to be a different crowd every time you checked it.

I had learned to scope the area well with my binoculars before I went down the long steps to the canal's locks and the levee where most people fished. By the time you got to them, they could easily just lay down their fishing pole and move away and avoid a fishing license violation because they could see you coming long before you got to them. So, I had learned to visually check the whole area with my binoculars and take notes before moving in to check licenses. It paid off on most occasions. This was a good spot to write a few citations on any given afternoon because a lot of people just wouldn't buy a license before going fishing.

On one occasion, I pulled my car into the parking area and moved to a pavilion to "glass" the area with my binoculars. On that particular day, all I saw was a man standing on the wall fishing for stripers in the river and what appeared to be his wife and little girl fishing in the canal. Actually, it was the woman fishing, and the little girl, who appeared to be about eight years old, was just playing nearby. I put my binoculars away and proceeded down the long steps and walkway.

By the time I got to the walkway approaching them, I noticed that the lady had moved away from the fishing pole and the little girl was holding the rod. Her daddy was casting for stripers from the wall about four feet above them both. I went to him first and asked for a license and he promptly produced one. After checking him, I thanked him and then moved to the lady, who was by then sitting several feet away from the little girl and her pole. When I asked her for a license she said she wasn't fishing. I then proceeded to explain to her how I had observed her with my binoculars from up on the observation platform before I ever started down the steps. Well, she knew then that she was caught, so she just said, "I ain't got no license." I asked her for some identification so that I could write her a citation, which is common procedure for a misdemeanor fishing without a license case. She informed me that she had left her purse at home and didn't have any ID. Well, she looked like a relatively honest lady, so I told her that I would just ask her some simple identification questions and fill out the ticket and be on my way.

All this time the husband kept fishing and appeared to be totally unconcerned about his wife's predicament. When I asked her what her name was, he spoke up and told her, "Don't tell him a damn thing," without ever even looking our way. Well, that chapped me off pretty badly, but I kept my cool and just asked her again what her name was. Before she could answer, he again said, "Don't tell him anything." I looked at her and said, "Lady, don't pay him any attention. Just tell me what I need to know and I'll be out of here in a few minutes." She responded, "I can't tell you my name. He won't let me." "Look, lady," I said, "if you don't tell me what I need to know, I'll have to take you to jail as a Jane Doe. Now you don't want that do you?" She began to get a terrified look in her eyes and said, almost crying, "You don't understand, mister, he'll hurt me if I don't do what he says." That statement made me so furious at him that I could hardly keep my composure. It was obvious to me that she was most likely a battered wife, or had been at one time. She was really frightened of him.

Well, at this point the little girl started crying and begging me not to take her mommy to jail. Wow! Talk about being in a tight, this was a losing proposition all the way around. Technically she was in violation of the law, but this situation was deteriorating really fast. I really didn't want to take this nice lady to jail, but I sure didn't have the same sentiments towards her cocky husband. I'd lock him up in a flash. Then, it hit me. He is the real culprit in this picture. I knew exactly what to do. I filled out the citation listing her name as Jane Doe and filled in what I could and made it a written warning. I tore it out of the book and gave her the warning copy of the citation and told her to have a nice day. Then I went to where Mr. Cocky was standing on the wall and said to him, "Let me see your license again." "What for?" he huffed. "Just let me see your fishing license," I demanded. He took the license out of his wallet and handed it to me. I got him off the wall and proceeded to write him a citation for interference with an officer in performance of his duties, a misdemeanor that carries a $1,000.00 fine. Well, he pitched a mortal fit about it as I slowly wrote the ticket out. I glanced over my shoulder at the lady who had a slight Mona Lisa-type smile on her face. The louder he got, the slower I wrote until I had to stop writing and tell him that if he opened his mouth one more time I was going to handcuff him and transport him to the county jail where he would spend the night. That was a promise I really wanted to keep, and I think he sensed that and so got quiet as a mouse. The way I see it, everything turned out pretty well; the lady was happy, the little girl was happy, I was happy, but Mr. Cocky was the only one who was having a bad day.

And when you think about it, he was the real bad guy in this situation. I told the lady that it would be a good idea if she got a license before she came fishing again. She just smiled and said OK.

About a month later, while patrolling that same river, I checked a boat with three men fishing from it. He was one of them, and I recognized him from the interference encounter. While checking these fellows, I asked them all for their fishing license except him. "I've already checked your license haven't I, sir?" I asked. "Yep," he replied without ever looking up. All in all, he was rather well mannered that day. I just wonder what he had to say after I pulled away.

- Chapter 9-
The Wood Narcs

By the very nature of the job, Rangers are out in the places where dopers, as they are called, grow their marijuana plants. Sometimes there will be just a small patch of "homegrown" dope planted by some good old boys growing their "wacky tobaccy" so they can make their own "left-handed" cigarettes. Then again, there are those commercial operations that are growing dope for the money. These are the dangerous ones who will kill you rather than look at you if they have the opportunity.

Rural south Georgia has become a haven for dope growers due to several factors that are in the favor of the growers. First, the warm climate and abundant rainfall are ideal for growing the illegal weed. Second, the location is ideal for transporting their illicit product since there are interstate highways that run nearby so their dope can be easily transported. Interstate 16, Interstate 95, and Interstate 75 are the main arteries leading north and west from the drug-laden locations in south Georgia and Florida. Third, rural law enforcement agencies are much lacking in manpower and equipment due solely to the fact a low population with an accompanying low tax base supports them. In short, there are just not enough funds to provide the needed manpower and equipment to catch these crooks.

Then, the last point is the real heartbreaker. Many of the small, rural communities can only pay their deputies and police officers a small minimum wage to do a very dangerous job. This opens the door for dopers to entice underpaid officers to take a bribe of big bucks to turn their backs or even escort them with their police cars so they won't get caught by another agency. It is always sad to hear about a sheriff, deputy, Ranger, trooper, or police officer being caught helping the bad guys with their unlawful enterprise. It gives all of law enforcement a bad name. For that reason, I am very proud of the sheriff's department of my local county and for their integrity that can't be bought. We have worked together on many occasions to see that the bad guys get their just dues.

There have been many incidents over the years where my fellow Rangers and I have had the opportunity to assist the local sheriff's departments with busting dopers. We caught a DC-8 airplane once that was loaded down with dope direct from Bogotá, Colombia. It landed on a remote landing strip in this rural county. The plane was seized, but the pilots got away when they lit a fire behind them to throw off the bloodhounds long enough for them to get away. Here are a couple of episodes that took place in Candler County, Georgia, of which I had the pleasure of being involved.

Story 1

I was on ATV (all terrain vehicle) patrol near the Ohoopee River one fine summer day when I came up behind a cabin that I knew to be vacant. A family from Savannah used it only on occasions. There was no electricity at the cabin. It was a quiet and peaceful little hide-away tucked in among old live oak trees laden with Spanish moss. There was a gentle slope from the back of the cabin that led down to the Ohoopee River. The Ohoopee was a favorite spot for redbreast bream fishing in the spring, so I would take my four-wheeler and patrol along the remote banks looking for fishermen.

As I approached the cabin from the rear, I noticed a pile of manure in the back yard that had been recently shoveled. As I looked around, I saw no plants, shrubs, trees, lawn, or any growing plants for which the manure might be used. I then noticed a path leading from the manure pile toward the woods and followed it for a little way. I soon came upon a well-fertilized patch of tall marijuana growing there. It had been well manicured and watered and was somebody's pride and joy. I backed out carefully and got on my ATV and left the area. I went directly to my vehicle, loaded my ATV onto it, and headed to the sheriff's office in town.

Once there, I met with the sheriff and we decided to call in a member of the Tri-County Drug Task Force to go to the location with us. When he arrived, I took a sheriff's department investigator and the task force officer to the site. I approached it from a different direction and hid my vehicle in a grove of small oaks. We then proceeded to the patch of dope and began to look around further. We found more than the one patch--much more. They had marijuana growing all over that property, and it looked like a pretty big operation. We had to catch this bunch.

The deputies and task force officers lay on the dope until the men came to work it, and they made the bust. It was a good one. Once they had made their arrests, they called us in with the four-wheelers to come look for more of the dope since they didn't want to leave too many signs in the area before. There was also a helicopter called in, and with the four-wheelers and chopper, we found still more dope growing. In all, four men were arrested and charged with manufacturing marijuana with intent to distribute. The men were all from Savannah, and search warrants were secured to search their residences in Chatham County. There was more dope found in the residence of the owner of the land.

The district attorney filed suit to have the Candler County property condemned since it was all used in the commission of a felony drug operation. In all, there were over 47 acres of prime riverfront land, a four-room cabin, a pickup truck, and several guns that were seized and condemned. The property was given to the Candler County government and later sold at auction, with the proceeds being placed in the general fund of the county. It was a good day for the county when that condemnation was awarded. But, you know, my property tax didn't go down one cent! But the bad guys had a bad day, and that made me have a good day.

Story 2

While on patrol one day, I stumbled across a small patch of "home-grown" marijuana. After telling the sheriff about it, I took a deputy into the area to show him, and a game plan was devised. The sheriff, being short-handed due to his small agency, needed Rangers to help catch the bad guys. We planned to lay on this dope patch until we caught somebody coming to it. It was about ready for harvest when I found it, so this shouldn't take long before we caught somebody. The dope patch was about five hundred yards off a paved county road just below a timber road that came within about 50 yards of the dope patch.

Another Ranger and I laid on it during the daylight hours, and two deputies laid on it at night. We had to be very careful getting to the area so we wouldn't be seen, but it was a very remote area with no houses nearby. We therefore had little trouble keeping it a secret. The usual day was spent lying in our concealed location on a poncho, taking turns watching the patch while the other napped or read a book. It was hot weather, so the gnats and heat kept the naps short. It reminded me of the way the Marine Corps often was. It seemed that everything was "hurry up and wait." This type of detail consisted of long hours of bore-dom followed by a short burst of surprise and excitement. The rewards would be seeing dopers taken off the active duty list and their noxious weed not reaching young people with its alluring charm and harm.

It was about mid-afternoon when we heard what sounded like mo-torcycles coming down the timber road and stopping in the woods nearby. They stopped just up the hill from the patch and shut their engines off. Within a couple of minutes, we saw what looked like two white males coming right toward the dope patch. They walked right up to it and began looking it over really closely. They walked between the rows and handled it gently as if inspecting the quality of the leaves. Soon they began walking back to their motorcycles.

I called the sheriff on my handheld walkie-talkie, and he was on the road coming our way. My radio was breaking up and I was having trouble getting the sheriff to understand what I was trying to tell him. Then I saw a tree nearby with just the right kind of limbs for climbing so up I scampered until I gained some elevation. There my radio should work better, so I gave it another try and the sheriff answered me. He said that he could understand me much more clearly now. I told him that there were two motorcycles coming out toward the paved road and it sounded like they turned north and headed in the direction of the interstate, which was about two miles away. I really hoped the sheriff would be able to intercept them before they got to the interstate highway or they would be gone for good.

He called me back in just a couple of minutes and told me that they had caught them and were holding them near the interstate on-ramp. One of the deputies came to our location and picked us up and we all headed to the county jail where the two suspects were being transported. The wrecker service picked up their motorcycles, and we all met at the jail.

The two were identified as a father and son team, and I knew them both. They were both game violators that I had trouble with over the years, but the son was still a juvenile. He was allowed to call his mother to come pick him up after we gathered the needed information for the juvenile court judge. When his mother answered the phone, he said to her, "Momma, me and daddy are in jail." You could just imagine her asking him what for and he was next heard to say, "We got caught by the ' Wood Narcs.'" He was talking about the Rangers, and we all laughed at the new name given to us. We became known after that as the "Wood Narcs." The deputies told everybody that the Rangers were now known as the "Wood Narcs," and so the moniker stuck.

That old man is dead now, and his son, no longer a juvenile, has been caught several times by me on hunting charges. I took him before the state court judge and he lost his hunting privilege in the state of Georgia for two years as well as paying a high fine for hunting on another person's land without permission. When the judge found out that he didn't have a job and that his wife would have to pay the fine, he reduced the fine to $25.00. The guy also admitted to the judge that he was a regular user of marijuana and liquor. The judge then made the young man go to mandatory drug treatment for a long period of time and ordered him, in open court, to get a job. The last account I had of him was that he is still giving the Rangers a hard time. I guess he will always be a hard case unless some judge gives him hard time in the pokey. The trouble is, prisons are crowded, and he will probably never get a jail term for a hunting violation. I wonder if he will ever learn his lesson.

It is not the intention of the Rangers to go out and look for dope, but when you find it you have to deal with it and help the local enforcement folks. So, I guess in a way we have earned the nickname of "Wood Narcs."

- Chapter 10-
Big Heart

The usual routine of the Rangers working Clarks Hill Lake during the summer was to be out there when a lot of people were on the lake. That would produce the desired effect of maximum exposure and would have a tremendous effect on bringing about voluntary compliance of the law, which is the ultimate goal of all law enforcement. But sometimes you go outside the norm just to see if something may be happening during the quieter times of the day. I mean, wouldn't it be interesting to go out on the lake say, during the wee hours of the morning, to see how much activity there may be at that time of the night? It was a time seldom worked by Rangers as a general rule.

With that in mind, I devised a plan. I would launch my patrol boat around midnight and work until daylight just to see what was happening at that time of the night. If there was no boating activity on the lake then I would know, but if there were a lot of violations taking place at that time of night, then we would be able to change our patrol tactics and deal with it. Rather than use one of the Rangers, I had planned to get one of the deputy Rangers to ride with me, mostly to keep me company. A good friend of mine was a deputy who just jumped at the prospect of working out there all night long.

We made our plans to meet at the boathouse at the state park and go out on the lake and see what was happening. I thought it would be best to go out into the middle of the Little River run, shut down, and just watch and listen. With my friend and a thermos of coffee in my boat, we hit the lake with much anticipation.

At first it looked like we might be wasting our time. There was scarcely anybody moving on the water. We checked a couple of boats that were headed in after fishing under the bridge, but for the most part it was like the Dead Sea--until about 3:00 A.M. You would be surprised how many people would cruise across the lake at night with no lights on board, and how many would ski in the darkness, which is illegal. One bunch was out there skiing in the nude, and was as drunk as termites in a yo-yo. Business was really picking up, and I had written several citations. Then, about 4:00 A.M. we were sitting quietly in the Little River run of the lake and I heard a dull hum of a distant outboard motor. We could see no lights, but it sounded like it was getting closer. I cranked my patrol boat, turned on the spotlight, and began to search the water surface. About 200 yards away was a pontoon boat running without lights, and it appeared to be loaded with partygoers.

As I pulled alongside I turned on my bow-mounted blue light for a moment just to let them know it was the Rangers approaching. Then, as I maneuvered my boat alongside theirs, I began to talk to the operator. In the course of my inspection, I was questioning him about his lack of running lights, and after securing his identification, I wrote him a citation for operating without lights after hours of darkness. All the time he was saying, "Hey, man, give me a break, man. Come on, man, have a heart, man." When I handed him that citation, I asked him to show us a life preserver for everybody on board. The best way to check such a rowdy crowd like this was to get everyone on board to hold up a life preserver at the same time. Well, they were sorely short of personal flotation devices, and as drunks will do, they tried to pull a fast one on me. A guy would hold up a life preserver and say, "Hey, man, here's mine," and then pass it behind his back to somebody else who would repeat the same lame statement. Once we had made a head count and a life preserver count we confirmed that they were short of having enough. I advised the operator that he was going to get another ticket. "Oh, man, have a heart man. Hey man, come on, man" was his plea. "I'm sorry, sir, but these are safety violations and I can't let them go," I said to him as I continued to write the second ticket.

Then, as I was about to finish up with him, I asked him to produce a fire extinguisher for inspection. After he and his crew had performed a frantic search for one, he confessed, "I guess we don't have one, man." "Well, I hate to do this, but I'll have to give you another ticket, sir," I said reluctantly. Then he just dropped his head and slumped into a pile of exasperation at the whole matter and said disgustedly, "Well, just stick a fork in my ass and turn me over, I am done!" At that, I just couldn't help myself. My partner and I almost fell out of the boat laughing. It was just so funny the way he said it and it being 4:00 o'clock in the morning probably added to the humor. After I recomposed myself, I told the guy that I would give him a verbal warning on that charge and just let it go this time. I just didn't have the heart to write that last ticket after he had said, "Hey, man, have a heart man" so earnestly.

My partner told everybody in the whole country about that little story of "Hey, man," and he gave me the nickname of "Big Heart." Until this day, 25 years later, he still calls me "Big Heart."

- Chapter 11-
Hey, Dummy!

I remember reading an article about some Tennessee Rangers putting a fully mounted white-tailed deer out in a field for potential ride-by shooters. Hunting from a motor vehicle and hunting from a public road are both illegal in Georgia, and the "dummy deer" idea caught on in my area as well. We also had a problem all over Georgia with people riding the country roads hunting on other people's land without permission.

It seemed that the genie was out of the bottle all over the country with many wildlife enforcement agencies engaging the dummy deer idea. All over this state, Rangers were acquiring deer and having taxidermists mount the whole animal. Then later, the idea expanded to include remote-control radios with servos mounted in the deer at vital points to make the animal move and therefore look more real. Mounting a whole deer and incorporating servos into strategic spots for natural movement is a very expensive undertaking. But all over the state there were sportsman organizations, private citizens, outdoor magazines, and the Rangers chipping in from their own pockets to get more of the illusive creatures into the field.

There was a group of anonymous sportsmen in my assigned county that contacted me and offered to supply all the needed items to make our own local remote-controlled "dummy deer" for my use in this area. The needed items included the deer cape, the remote radio-control box with servos, and even the money to pay for the taxidermists' work to make the project come to fruition. I was delighted that there were local sportsmen who wanted to make it a reality for me so I could better catch some of these people who were riding the roads and taking shots at deer standing in woods and fields. In the past, if I saw deer standing in a field or pasture I would hide my vehicle nearby and hope to take advantage of the natural decoys. It worked most of the time if the deer would cooperate and stay in the area long enough.

I had worked closely with the taxidermist as to the placement and use of the servos. He wanted to be able to make one of the ears move, but ear movement was difficult to duplicate in a natural manner, so we decided to mount one of the tiny motors in the tail and another in the neck. When it was all finished, my deer would wiggle his tail or move his head from side to side with the movement of a joystick from up to a hundred yards away. I was finally ready to set it up in the field and see if we got any takers.

One of the early problems we ran into was the legal issue of entrapment. But most of the district attorneys and state court solicitors agreed that it was not entrapment if the decoy was set up in a natural setting and not out in direct line of sight so as to entice or lure someone into doing something they wouldn't have done otherwise. Legal mumbo jumbo aside, we just made the deer visible to those who were looking for one. If you were an innocent motorist, you would most likely not even see the decoy. Finding the right spot was not an easy task and once found, setting up the decoy and placing the contact person was another task where stealth and safety were both considered to the extreme degree. We wouldn't move the head or wiggle the tail unless we had a prospective violator who was trying to decide if it was the real thing or not.

Here's how the ideal setup would most often be. The decoy would be set up in the edge of the woods or a field about seventy-five to a hundred yards from the road. Down the road a ways would be the jump car or truck hidden off the side of the road. There were usually one or two Rangers in the vehicle waiting for the order from the spotter to come quickly to the site. Then, in the woods or weeds across the road from the decoy would be the spotter who would be equipped with a walkie talkie, a video camera, and a camouflage covering. The whole idea was to see the violators without being seen and get a video movie of the violation for court. Sometimes we would just stand behind a big tree or maybe get in an old abandoned house or barn and out of the line of fire.

Once the decoy was set up, the excitement or boredom would commence. Sometimes you might go for hours without any "takers" and then all of a sudden the brake lights of a vehicle would come on and the spotter would put the jump car on alert. The call would come: "All right, listen up, we might have a customer; get ready." If the suspect were to shoot at the decoy, the person in the jump truck or car would hear the shot about the same time the call came from the spotter: "Come on! Come on! He just shot! Come on quick, it's a blue truck with two occupants." "We're rolling," the call would come back. Then the dummy deer, with a little help from the game warden, would catch the illegal shooters. Most of the time the suspects would just laugh at the whole affair and most often would say, "I've heard about that thing, but I thought I could tell the difference." The problem for the violators was that it was a real deer, just not alive. I had mastered the movement of the tail. With a quick flick of the joystick, the tail would flick like the deer was swishing away a fly. It looked real. Now, here are some stories of real incidents we encountered with the "dummy deer."

Once, we caught a guy in Jenkins County with the decoy, and about a week later we caught the same guy with the same "dummy deer" in Bulloch County. The judge just asked him if he would ever learn his lesson. We made a believer out of that guy. From then on every real deer got a new lease on life because the bad guys would think they were decoys. That was the whole idea.

Then there was the time when I got a call from a man who was a member of a hunting club in the northern part of my county. He told me of a particular field where an eight-point buck and two does had been killed by road hunters, without permission of course. He asked me if we could use the dummy deer and catch them. I told him that we would give it a try one day soon. As it turned out, the decoy, being the hot item it was with the Rangers, was in high demand in all the counties around. Then, one day about ten days after the complaint, Sergeant Biggers and I went into the area and looked for the perfect spot. The field he had told me about wasn't a good place to set up in because there was not a good hiding spot for the jump car. So, we went about a mile down the road and set up in another spot. I was the spotter and Sergeant Biggers was in the jump car. I had set up in an old house that was used by a local farmer to store hay in. I had the video camera on a tripod facing out of the window, and I had the walkie-talkie ready. I could see the decoy, and there was a slight embankment between the road and my position.

As I watched the road, a small truck stopped and a man got out. He looked up and down the road and pulled a rifle out of the truck. He laid it across the top of the truck and POW! He shot at the decoy. One shot was all he took. Once he had taken his shot, he just dropped his head and laid the gun in the seat of the truck and went back and sat on the tailgate of the truck. He knew he was caught. In the meantime, I called Biggers, who was there in a little less than a minute. I watched as he got the suspect's identification from him and asked him to follow him back to his hiding place so he could write the tickets. We usually did that so we could be working the decoy sooner and not have any more activity at the scene than was necessary.

As Sergeant Biggers got into his car and the violator got into his truck and turned around to follow him, Biggers called me on the radio and asked me if I knew a Mr. Robert Thomas. I quickly recognized the name as the man who had been our complainant. When I told Sergeant Biggers about that, he told me that the man had asked him to promise him he wouldn't tell Sergeant Hethcox about this no matter what, and so Biggers told him, "I promise I won't tell him." He didn't have to tell me because I saw it all. It was a long time before I saw the man, and he acted like he couldn't look me in the eye. I acted as if nothing had happened, and I think he never knew that I knew it was he. Like I said, sometimes truth is stranger than fiction.

Many times we would be watching the decoy and somebody would spot it thinking it was a real deer. They would stop and blow their horn or beat on the side of the truck to scare it away. Most of the time I would have to step out and show myself, whistle or get their attention somehow and ask them if they would move on. They would usually just laugh and say, "I thought that was y'all."

One night Sergeant Biggers had the decoy set up in the field on the other side of the road from his position. About midnight a truck came by and turned into the field to shine the field with his headlights. That was a practice many night hunters used instead of shining a spotlight out the window. They could always claim they were just turning around. Well, this guy saw the decoy and began driving toward it at a high rate of speed. He kept going faster and faster until he hit the decoy and busted it all to pieces. Sergeant Biggers arrested the guy for destruction of state property, and the judge made him replace the decoy deer and pay a fine. That was a strange one for the record books, night hunting with a truck.

On most of the details I would choose to be the spotter, and work the decoy and video camera. That gave me the opportunity to see the whole thing as it happened. The jump car would have to go on my word. So, to me the best duty was working the decoy.

I remember one day Sergeant Biggers and I were working on the county line area and he was standing behind a big pine tree with the camera. On that particular day, I was the jump car. After a while an old Ford truck came down the road occupied by two brothers. When they spotted the decoy deer, they stopped almost beside where he was standing. He had to call on the radio with a loud whisper. I was on alert. Then, the man on the passenger side stepped out and laid the shotgun barrel across the hood of the truck and took a shot with 12-gauge double-ought buck shot. When the deer didn't move or go down, the man slowly turned around looking for a game warden. Biggers stepped out from behind the tree and with the camera on his shoulder said, "Just stand still right there, a Ranger is on the way." He just laughed and told his brother, "I told you it was probably that dummy deer." They seemed to be having the time of their life until the judge laid the fine on them; then it wasn't so funny.

Hunting from a motor vehicle and hunting from a public road are a very dangerous business, and hunting without permission is downright unethical as well as illegal. We had a problem with those violations before the decoy deer project came into existence, but thanks to some donations and old-fashioned Ranger ingenuity, the problem was brought under control. We still have a reputation of having that decoy deer out everywhere. The truth is that it got such a positive reputation that most of the road riders quit doing it and it finally got to where we had a hard time catching bad guys with it. Rangers still use it on night details and will put reflective tape on the decoy's eyes so they will shine if a light hits them. That looks real, and almost every time will draw a shot of fire. Rangers have to be extremely careful where they place a decoy so that no one's house, barn, or livestock is in the potential line of fire.

A shooter in an old chartreuse van stopped to shoot at the decoy deer one day. When the Rangers drove up with their blue lights and siren going, the shooter got so excited that he shot a hole in the floorboard of the van. Many times we have approached a vehicle that was stopped for night hunting or road shooting and as the occupants tried to quickly unload their firearm, it would go off and kill their truck. Fortunately, no one has shot himself or herself, but their ears will probably ring for the rest of their lives.

One winter afternoon we were set up with the decoy deer in a very remote spot in lower Bulloch County in an area called Bulloch Bay. A little compact truck came down the road and stopped adjacent to the decoy. The driver slowly rolled his window down and out came a .22 semiautomatic rifle. Those little rifles will hold a handful of cartridges and this guy was trying to put one of those .22 rounds into that deer. He kept taking very careful aim and shooting round after round after round. He was so engrossed in what he was doing he didn't even notice Sergeant Biggers approaching from the other side of the road. The sergeant walked up to the passenger side window and tapped on the glass. When the guy turned around he saw this big game warden peering at him through his window, and Sergeant Biggers said, "You can quit shooting now, I don't think he's going to fall." At that, the guy turned almost solid white and nearly passed out. I do believe he wet his pants, but after he gained his composure, he got his just rewards for his efforts.

- Chapter 12-
The Still

Illegal whiskey goes by many names; among them are moonshine, white lightning, who-hit-John, corn squeezins, and firewater just to name a few. In decades gone by, white liquor was the favorite of the back-hills folks and was considered none of the government's business if country folks made a little "rheumatiz medicine." But the Department of Revenue thought it was the government's business if people made and sold untaxed whiskey. So the hide-and-seek game was on, with the "revenuers" trying to find it, while the bootleggers tried to hide it.

Moonshiners, or bootleggers as they are sometimes called, devised clever ways to hide the manufacture and distribution of their intoxicating brew, and the law enforcement officers developed better and more sophisticated ways to find and destroy these means of producing moonshine. The old method of walking the backwoods is the best way to find them and deal with them on the spot. That's where the Rangers come in.

Usually finding liquor stills is not the job of the Conservation Rangers but the very nature of their job places them out in the boonies where stills are to be found. It is not unusual for a Ranger to find a still while walking the woods looking for baited deer and turkey stands. Many times the local sheriff's department is the primary agency in locating stills and dealing with them because the number of revenue agents is not nearly enough to search the woods for illegal whiskey. So it stands to reason that the wise sheriff will seek the aid of his local Conservation Ranger to at least keep his eyes open for the possibility of running across a still.

In more recent years, there have been fewer and fewer liquor stills while the manufacture of homegrown marijuana, also known as pot, has increased. Another problem that is surfacing in recent times is the "cooking" of crack cocaine and, more dangerously, the clandestine methamphetamine laboratory, or "meth lab." Those things are extremely dangerous and highly explosive, not to mention some of the most unstable and toxic chemicals that can be imagined. That is some really bad stuff. It makes the old-fashioned moonshine operation look like a play school.

Rangers have found it all as they walk the woods. It is not unusual for a Ranger to come across illegal whiskey or drugs and immediately realize that he or she is in grave danger. These operations many times are surrounded with booby traps or armed guards. So it is very serious when you stumble across dope or whiskey being made or grown.

One such incident happened to me a few years back in rural Candler County, Georgia. I was walking the woods on a complaint about baited deer stands in a certain patch of woods across the road from a remote country church. The complainant said that he had been in those woods on his four-wheeler and had seen corn sacks where someone had been putting out deer feed at tree stands. Well, I don't know if this guy knew there was a still in the area or not. Sometimes one moonshiner will give a tip to the law enforcement folks about another moonshiner's operation. By doing this, he can remove his competition without his name being used or even coming up. Many of these "calls" come in anonymously.

I knew this guy personally, and his information was usually right on target. So I headed to the area and hid my patrol vehicle behind the church in the woods. I crossed the road trying not to make tracks in the fresh dirt that would be a tip off to an illegal hunter.

You see that's the trouble with getting set in your mind about what you intend to find and you tend to look for what you expect to find. Many times a Ranger will walk right up on something that he or she is not expecting simply because they are looking for something related to game and fish. You have to be careful not to fall into this trap of working with blinders on. At least, that's what I called it. We get used to looking for things in our scope of operation and become lax in being on guard for something that may be much more danger-ous. Rangers have to guard against getting set in their thinking and must keep an open mind and an open eye to those things that they don't expect. You can run across almost anything out there today and you have to be on your best vigilance for the unexpected.

As I crossed the road, I merged into the woods and began to walk the boundary between the open woods and the thicket that bordered the swamp nearby. The woods across the road from the church had a gentle downward slope that ran into a swampy thicket. When I reached the thicket, I went alongside it slowly looking for tree stands or anything that might evidence that I was on the right trail. I kept the thicket on my left and the open woods on my right and walked along that boundary looking into the thicket and up the slope toward the road.

It was early summer and it was a warm and humid day. Then, all of a sudden, I smelled marijuana growing. You can smell it in the green plant stage if the breeze and humidity and proximity are all working in your favor. I smelled dope growing, but I couldn't see it anywhere. I figured it must be in the thickets because I could see into the open woods to my right and there was none there. Being cautious, I drew my sidearm and slowly walked along looking for anything that appeared out of place.

I walked along the thicket boundary, which curved around to the left. Then I saw a large rusty looking steel container about the size of a trash dumpster. Do you see what happened here? I went from looking for baited deer stands, to looking for marijuana, to seeing a liquor still all in a matter of a few minutes. That is what I was talking about when I said you have to keep an open mind when you are patrolling.

Upon seeing this big metal structure, I didn't realize at first what I was looking at. Then it occurred to me that I was looking at a liquor still. There were several propane bottles lying around the site, and you could tell there had been quite a bit of foot traffic around the area because the ground was bare. I was looking at what is known as a "groundhog still." It was set up on blocks and under it was a makeshift gas burner made of copper tubing with holes bored into it and connected to a propane gas cylinder. There was a round opening on the top of the still about the size of a manhole cover with a burlap bag covering the top to keep leaves and bugs out of the mash.

I could smell the mash working off and removed the burlap enough to look inside the still. It was about three-fourths full of water, corn, sugar, yeast, and some odd ingredients I didn't recognize. There were all the makings for a liquor cooking just as soon as it reached the best work-off. I saw a piece of PVC pipe running from the still down toward the swamp for a water supply. It was really a nasty operation, and I knew I had to hurry up and get out of there. I had to go tell the sheriff what I had found. I sure didn't want to get caught in there around the still, so I slipped out of the woods and back to my car as stealthily as I could and drove into town. I was careful not to use a radio because there were so many scanners in the county, and I didn't want to tip anybody off about what I had found. I had to tell the sheriff in person.

When I arrived at the sheriff's department, I met with the sheriff and two of his finest deputies. We decided that for the sake of professional courtesy we would call in the revenue agent to be included in the plans of how to deal with it. While we waited on the agent, I filled in the sheriff and deputies on where it was located and possible hiding places for a vehicle. When the agent arrived, we decided that one of the deputies would drop the three of us off from an unmarked vehicle and we would walk in to where the still was. I would lead them into the area and we could see it and make a game plan on how to work it.

So one of the deputies dropped us off about a half mile from the church behind an old abandoned barn and we walked through the woods and right to the still. We watched for tripwires, cameras, and such and tried not to make any signs that we had been there. The revenue agent would be able to tell us how far along the work-off of the mash was and the approximate cook date. The agent walked down the trail where the PVC pipe went into the swamp and found a Honda water pump on the other end setting on a stump. They would just fire it up and pump water up to the still as needed. It was really nasty, mosquito-infested water, but they were using it to make liquor. No wonder they call it "rot-gut" whiskey.

Having seen all we needed to see and making our best judgments about the cook-off date, we promptly left before we were seen in the area. We had no idea when someone might come to the still, and we surely didn't want to be caught in there. We walked back through the woods at least a half a mile to the pickup point and just as we got to the old barn, the revenue agent discovered that his badge was missing. The agents wore plain clothes with their badge clipped on their belt. It was a big gold badge, and it was lost! Holy cow! I could just see it lying beside the still face up like a big old

Cadillac hubcap. We had to go back and find it, so we began to backtrack to the still.

We made it all the way back to the still looking as we went back over the exact steps we had just walked looking for that badge. Finally, we arrived back at the still, and the revenue agent began to retrace his steps around the still. There it was! He found it in the trail of the PVC pipe that led down to the water supply. It was lying right in the path face up in the sun and shining like a gold mirror. Whew! That was a close one. If one of the bootleggers had seen that badge, it would have been over. We were glad we had found it and once again made our way back to the pickup point behind the old barn. The pickup deputy was waiting for us and wondering what took so long. We hadn't taken walkie-talkies in with us because we wanted to maintain radio silence anyway. After explaining the whole story to him, we all had a good laugh and went back to town to finalize our game plan.

The local sheriff's department was a small one with only a sheriff and three deputies at that time, and it was obvious the sheriff needed some help on this one if we were to lay surveillance on the still until we caught the bad guys. The state revenue agents bowed out of the surveillance part since they had other duties that kept them busy. An old retired federal revenue agent had told me that they didn't lay on a still. They would hide a thermocouple near the burner and bury the wire under the ground in a shallow line away from the still. Then they would tack the wire up the backside of a tree and attach it to a transmitter. The heat from the burner activated the thermocouple when the moonshiners were cooking off the mash, and a constant signal would emit from the small transmitter. Then, they would come quickly to the still and catch them while they were cooking it. Well, that all sounded great, but we didn't have that sophisticated gadgetry, so we had to do it the old-fashioned way...we had to lay on it.

It was decided that we would lay on it 24 hours a day until we caught them. The sheriff would put his two best deputies on it for twelve hours during the night and two Rangers would lie on it for twelve hours during the daytime until we caught them. This went on for over a week and no one had come to the area and nothing had happened. We wondered if someone had a tip that we were lying on it. Everything was quiet about it as far as we could tell but for some reason, they hadn't come to it. It was now past time to cook it, so we had to devise another plan.

We decided to back off of it for a few days to see if anybody came to it and then slip back in for another look. If they didn't cook it soon, then we knew they had made us. When we went back into the area we discovered that the still was gone! They had moved it, but where? After we had made a thorough search of the surrounding area, we found it in the woods behind the church on the other side of the road. What luck! We got back on the job, and in two days the guy was caught. Here's how the bust went down.

It was early in the morning just before 6:00 A.M. Shift change time was about 6:00 A.M., so if the guy had come a little later it would have messed us up, and we might have been caught ourselves. Think about it, we were trying to catch a guy and, at the same time, trying not to get caught or be seen by the bad guy. At just about 5:45 A.M., he backed his pickup truck right up to the still. His truck was loaded with fifty-pound bags of sugar, and on the seat of the truck was a box of yeast. He was getting ready to sweeten up the mash and make another run.

He had made a cooking after he moved the still behind the old church, and we had found part of his stash of moonshine. It was two plastic, five-gallon containers of clear moonshine hidden beside the road where he could drop by and make a pickup or pour off a gallon or two and go make a sale. The guy that we caught was an old moonshiner from way back. His father before him had been a moonshiner, and this man was raised carrying sugar back into the river swamp as a small boy.

Back in the interrogation room at the sheriff's department, I asked him why he had decided to make moonshine whiskey and he just said, "Everybody's got to do something for a living. I just don't like carpentry work." He was found guilty of manufacturing and selling illegal, untaxed whiskey and was sentenced to the state penitentiary for two years and probation. I guess it's the age-old story of trying to make money the illegal way instead of the honest way: old-fashioned hard work.

I never did get back to that area where I had smelled the marijuana growing just before I saw the still. I think this guy was making hooch and growing dope at the same time. We never did catch him with the pot, but he didn't get away with his illegal ways.

The revenue agents wanted to blow up the still with dynamite, but the sheriff wanted to let the county maintenance shop have the plate steel. He said it was easy to destroy something, but it made more sense to make good use of it. That plate steel is expensive and the county could make good use of it. So the county maintenance shop boys came and cut it up and moved it away to the county shop.

There was a lot of media there the day we made the bust, and the news of the bust was on the Savannah television stations that evening as well as in the local papers. I was proud to have been a part of this operation, but at the same time I was glad it was over. Now we could all return to our routine (?) duties.

- Chapter 13-
Hook, Line and Stinker

About the time you think you've seen it all, you realize you haven't. And may I say there are some real "nuts" in this world, and every once in a while you find one that makes you wonder what makes him tick. He's just a bubble left of plumb, or, his elevator doesn't go all the way to the top. You know the type. Sometimes they go fishing! And I had the opportunity to check the license of such an individual one summer day on a creek tributary of Clarks Hill Lake.

I was patrolling the lake one beautiful Saturday afternoon and having a really great day. I came upon a creek that comes into the lake and I went into the mouth of the creek with my 17-foot patrol boat. The water was backed up into the creek and was navigable for a long way. As I made my way up this creek, I began to notice that I was going much farther than I ever thought possible in that big boat. This particular creek comes under a highway bridge about a half a mile from the lake and is a favorite fishing spot, being easily accessible from the road. As long as I had plenty of water and could maneuver, I kept going slowly just to see how far I could go.

At last I caught sight of the bridge and took my binoculars and could see one guy sitting on the bank under the bridge alone, fishing. Now you have to understand he didn't see or hear me coming nor could he have known that any game warden would be coming from that direction. There was also no one at the bridge except him at that very rural spot. He was happy and content as he fished under the bridge in the creek.

When I finally made it to where he was, I pulled my boat up to the bank, exited it and tied up so I could check his license. He appeared to be in his twenties and never took his eyes off his "float" while I made my approach to him. I made the usual greeting, small talk, and such that I always did, but he seemed mesmerized by his task at hand and still didn't take his eyes off his float. I then asked him for his license to which he replied, "I ain't fishing." "Well, just what do you call yourself doing?" I asked. "Nothing," said he. Well, I might look dumb, but I didn't just fall off a pumpkin wagon, and this jaybird wasn't about to pull one over on me. I could just see myself getting ready to take this smart guy to jail.

"All right, fellow," I said, "knock off the nonsense and let me see a license or you are going to be in trouble, do you understand?" "Really, sir," he said, "I ain't fishing." "Well, what do you call yourself doing?" I asked abruptly. At that point, he slowly pulled his line out of the water and there in his hand was a fishing line complete with a red and white float. About a foot below the float was a rock! That's right, a plain old roadside rock tied to a piece of line with a float above it. There was no rhyme or reason to it, and there was also no hook. He was a nut!

Now, friends, he couldn't have been pulling one over on me because he couldn't have known I was coming. I finally concluded that he was just enjoying the great outdoors on the economy plan -- no bait, no hook, no license, no smell, no cleaning fish later, but really enjoying his afternoon "rock fishing." I bid that strange dude a good day and left him intently watching his rock float. I told you earlier that truth is stranger than fiction, didn't I? Well, this is one for the record book. As I drove away I wondered what was going on between his ears.

- Chapter 14 -
Hawks, Eagles and Stolen Trucks

Several times during my career I have planned one thing and something else would come up unexpectedly. Such was the case one evening when I had called my wife on the phone and told her that I would be home as soon as I finished teaching the hunter safety class I was working on. It was a weekday class and I was to finish early that afternoon. I had planned to go home and just relax with my family afterwards. My wife told me she would have supper waiting for me and we planned to have a rare "sit-down-together" meal. That was rare indeed.

About the time the corporal and I finished and had dismissed the students, I got a call from the sheriff's office in Evans County, just south of us. They said there was a man out in the county that was reportedly holding an eagle in a pen and was going to take it to south Florida the next morning to sell it. The corporal and I went down there to check it out. An informant had told the sheriff's deputy about the eagle in the pen and the man's plan to sell it in Florida. It had to be checked out because it was reported that he was moving out before daylight the next morning. The informant said he would be towing a trailer loaded down with goats, chickens, turkeys, and of course, the eagle.

I drove my car close to the residence and hid it in the woods nearby. The corporal and I then walked through the woods, crossed a couple of creeks and fences, and finally made our way to the man's place. This eagle pen was supposed to be behind his house around the barnyard area. The barn was about 100 or so feet behind the residence and it was junky and brushy between the house and barn.

We approached from the woods behind his barn and crawled up to the barnyard. We couldn't believe our eyes. There were pens and junk vehicles all around the barnyard. There were several species of livestock penned up and ready to be transported. There were goats, chickens of all varieties, turkeys, pigeons, and one little chicken coop with a hawk in it. It was a red-tailed hawk and a beautiful specimen of one at that. There was no eagle. The hawk was so big it had probably been mistaken as an eagle. Possession of this hawk was also a violation of state and federal law, and interstate transportation of it was a federal violation also.

As we slipped around the barnyard looking into coops and pens, we noticed something odd. There were also several vehicles in the barnyard area. They were not junks but new-model trucks and cars. There was one truck that was only a year old, but it had no engine in it. It was not wrecked, so that wouldn't account for it being parked there. It was up on blocks with the tires and wheels missing. Over to the side was a Mercedes sedan that appeared to be about four or five years old with nothing apparently wrong with it. We decided to jot down the vehicle identification numbers of these vehicles and run them on the Georgia Crime Information Center (GCIC) and the National Crime Information Center (NCIC) when we got back to the sheriff's office. If they were stolen, it would show up on the computer check.

By the time all this was done and we had made our way out of the area and back to my car, it was already dark. I still hadn't thought about my supper promise to my wife. There was just too much going on, and besides, she knew my job was like that. How many times had I gone out the door with good intentions to return at a certain time, and something important had come up that kept me occupied until the next day without a chance to call home? That's what it was like being a Ranger, and she knew that. I just never knew from one minute to the next what I might get caught up in. She understood that. She was a good Ranger wife.

When we got back to the sheriff's office we ran those numbers on the computer and BAM, we got a hit! Both of them came back as stolen vehicles. All of a sudden the hawk wasn't the more important aspect of the barnyard. This guy had been stealing vehicles or at least he was in possession of them.

The sheriff wanted us to take his deputy back into the barnyard to get a better look at these vehicles and see if there might be some other contraband or stolen property there. We took him back there the same way we had made our way there the first time, except now it was totally dark and it took longer. By the time we got back to the sheriff's office the second time, it was nearly midnight.

We were beyond the scope of a Ranger's duties so we called the Georgia Bureau of Investigations (GBI) agent at home and woke him up. During our conversation with him there arose a question about the legality of our find as to whether it had been a lawful search. It took us, the GBI agent, the assistant district attorney, and the sheriff's department most of the night to come to the conclusion that the Rangers were well within our authority and that the search was legal. The courts hold that Rangers in their unique type of enforce-ment have more latitude with the constitutional guidelines than the average enforcement officer due to the nature and scope of their job. Rangers check people on their property all the time within the authority of law. This was accepted by the courts, and, therefore, the discovery was lawful. It took the legal beagles most of the night searching case files to come to that conclusion, but now we were ready to set up our surveillance and get ready for the takedown.

There were several roads that led out from this man's residence, and we weren't sure which road he would take, so the game plan was to cover them all. We had enough people, so we all took up our locations in the wee hours of the morning and watched for the man to make a move. We would take him down on the road and charge him with possession and transportation of the illegal wildlife and then serve the search warrants on his house and barn area. We would have him then. The trap was laid, and here we sat.

With me in my car were the chief deputy, the GBI agent, and the corporal. It was about 5:00 A.M, and we were just talking about how wives worry and fret about their husbands when they don't come home at a certain time. I listened to them as they talked about their worrying wives and incidents when their wives would call them and embarrass them on the job. I was gloating inside and about to burst to tell them that my little wife had "never" done that. Then, when I got a chance to get my word in, I told them that after 15 years of law-enforcement work, my wife had NEVER called anybody worrying about me. Well, as the words were still hanging in the cool, quiet morning air, the radio dispatcher at the sheriff's office called, "Evans County to 519." I tensed up. The guys in the car began to tease me and ask me if my wife was checking up on me. Then, reluctantly, I answered the dispatcher and he replied, "519, I have your wife on the phone and she wants to know if you're OK." The car erupted in laughter, and I was thankful for the darkness that hid my blushing face. Boy, was I embarrassed! After all these years of patience and understanding, she had chosen this particular morning, this particular hour, this particular minute to call and check up on me, and the timing was just awful. I had just run off my big mouth in a braggadocios manner and she happened to call at that particular moment. "10-4, Evans County. Advise her I'm OK and I'm not sure when I'll be home," I replied.

You can imagine how quickly that story traveled through the halls of law enforcement and my friends had a good laugh at my expense. Well, we caught our man about daybreak and served the search warrant. The guy got some prison time on this one and we got a feather in our caps for another job well done. I was proud to take part in that bust.

When I got home, I told my wife about the timing of her call and how I had just bragged about how she never calls me. She said, "Honey, I could just see you lying in some ditch somewhere wondering if I would call somebody to come and help you." I certainly couldn't blame her for that, and I sure was proud to have a wife who cared enough to check. It could have been the way she imagined it. You just never know.

- Chapter 15-
The 'Chile' Was Gone!

While working on Clarks Hill Lake in the mid-1970s, my partner and I were patrolling near the dam one beautiful summer day when we spotted what looked like two South Carolina Rangers in a boat coming our way. They were motioning for us to stop and come to them. I was driving our boat and noticed that they had what appeared to be a black female passenger riding with them.

As we came alongside them, the one closest to me said they were glad to see us. I asked what was going on, and they told us that there had apparently been a drowning on the Georgia side of the lake. The state line ran down the center of the old Savannah River run at the dam, and we were out near the middle of the lake at the state line. After filling us in on their sketchy details, they told us that this person was riding in a boat in Georgia waters when a passenger fell overboard. The big Carolina Ranger said, "This is yours now," and they acted like they were happy to be rid of the lady. I was embarrassed for the lady because of the way these men were acting toward her and referring to her as a "this." She stood up to get into our boat, and I handed her a life preserver and said, "Watch your step, ma'am," at which the South Carolina Ranger replied, "That ain't no ma'am." "What do you mean?" I asked. You've got to understand that I was extremely naive back then and had not a clue as to what he meant. "Well," he said matter-of-factly, "This here is a man, and he's all yours." "A MAN! " I exclaimed. Then my partner spoke up and commanded, "Get in this boat and watch your step; sit down back there." At that, the South Carolina boys bid us a good day and told us they were glad this one was in Georgia. Now the ball was in our court, so to speak, and we began to question our witness.

We went to a nearby marina and placed a phone call to the sheriff's office and the chief deputy came to the marina where we were. We placed our peculiar witness in the deputy's patrol car, and he and I went to the Carolina side where two more of the ill-fated crew waited at a state park. My partner stayed with the boat at the marina and summoned our supervisor to come to the scene. There were, in all, about four female impersonators that had taken a party ride with some soldiers from nearby Fort Gordon Army base.

Upon arriving at the state park on the South Carolina side, the other two people were waiting, and quite happy to see us show up with their other friend. We brought all three of them over to the Georgia side, to the sheriff's office for questioning. The following is a brief synopsis of their statements.

They had met some soldiers from Fort Gordon who had invited them to go partying with them on the lake. We never were able to identify the soldiers or even know how many there were. There was booze and who-knows-what-all on board and off they went on their ride on the lake. From what they all said, we gathered that none of them was at all familiar with the lake and had no idea where the incident had happened.

Apparently, one of the occupants had been standing at the rear of the boat near the transom and had fallen backwards overboard into the clear green deep without making a sound. No one knew how much time had transpired between the victim falling overboard and their discovery of his/her disappearance. The witness told us, "When I looked back to say something to Rachael, the chile' was gone!" When I asked how old the child was, I was told that the victim was in his/her thirties. I inquired why he/she called it a child, he/she just looked at me and said, "That's how we talk, honey."

All in all, this was a really weird bunch of people. They weren't very reliable as witnesses and what's worse, no one knew where Rachael had fallen overboard. Heck, I couldn't even get them to tell me what Rachael's real name was. When I questioned the one about Rachael's sex, he just said that God had made a mistake at Rachael's birth and she just straightened it out. I had never encountered anybody like this, and I couldn't believe what I was hearing. None of them knew where they were at any given time they were on the water. They said they were turned around the whole time they were in the boat. Not being familiar with the lake, they weren't much help with trying to pinpoint the location where the body went down.

When they discovered they had a passenger missing overboard, the soldiers took them to the South Carolina side to a state park. After they unloaded the whole bunch, they sped away. They didn't stick around to help or take responsibility for anything.

There was just no way to get any leads on who the soldiers were since their riders claimed they had never known them before this day. Now we had to try to determine where the victim had gone down. That too was a dead-end street. We knew that there would be no usual dragging/diving operations to recover the body since we didn't have a location in which to look. Clarks Hill is a pretty big lake and somewhere out there on the bottom of this abyss was a dead black male who was dressed like a black female. Now I began to see why the South Carolina Rangers wanted to drop this hot potato in our laps. This was definitely one for the books. I had never run into a situation quite like this before nor have I ever seen anything like it since.

Early every morning after that I would take my boat and ride the shoreline and crisscross the lake looking for a floating body. That's what a drowned victim will do unless the body is caught on some structure or entangled on the bottom. When the body gasses begin to amass, the body will swell and rise to the top like a big float. The closer it gets to the top the faster it will rise until it "pops" up. It was a bad duty, no doubt about it, and I just wanted to find the body and be done with this sordid affair. Then, about ten days after the incident, Rachael popped up out in the open waters about a half a mile from the dam. A boater riding in the area spotted the body floating and called us. This man had heard about it on the news and knew what it was when he first saw it.

Having worked literally hundreds of drownings over the years, I have concluded that people just don't think about how dangerous being on the water can be. Most of the victims' bodies that I have recovered have been young people, many of them teenagers and some children. As a father of three, every time I would pull a drowned victim from the water, I would think of this person's parents or loved ones. I knew they would be heartbroken and never see them again in this life. Years later, I still have thoughts of some of the victims whose bodies I have recovered. In my memories I can still see the weeping family members on the bank when the body is recovered.

Although I disagreed with the chosen lifestyle of Rachael and his/her friends, I still can't help but feel sorry for them at the great loss of life and the prospects of eternity.

- Chapter 16-
Ducking the Man

Duck-hunting techniques vary across the United States due primarily to the flyways, species in a given area, habitat, and local preferences. Down in rural southeast Georgia, the wood duck is the most prevalent duck since there are no appreciable flyways nearby except along the Georgia coast. These little ducks are considered by most to be locally grown ducks, but they do migrate. Locals have called them "summer ducks" and "woodies" for eons, I guess, and they have developed their own ways of taking them. The limit was usually two ducks per day on woodies and any good ole boy would tell you, "That ain't enough to make the pot stink."

Morning hunting is almost unheard of in the coastal plains of Georgia, and hunting after hours is an accepted practice among most locals. I remember when I first transferred to south Georgia and went out to work duck hunting like I had done upstate. I tried to locate early morning shoots to no avail. That's when I learned that these folks prefer evening shooting. And I do mean evening!

Everybody knows that ducks don't start coming into the roost ponds in the evening until about a half an hour or so after shooting hours end. It's almost impossible to shoot legally in the late afternoon. That doesn't seem to hinder some of the local violators because they don't usually care what the shooting hours are anyway. Their style is "hit and run" shoots, and they almost never shoot the same ponds more than once. You can see that in order to find one of these shoots you have to be lucky and quick. You have to be lucky to be close enough to the pond when the shooting starts because it doesn't usually last long, and fast enough to locate it and get positioned in order to make the "bust."

Well, once in a while the Rangers hit everything just right and usually make several arrests for multiple waterfowl violations for their troubles. And then, once in a while everything just really works out for the Ranger who is ready for anything and is clever enough to take advantage of the situation.

Such was the case late one fall afternoon on a remote, long cypress pond in rural Bulloch County. One of the corporals and I were close to the area when we heard the first shots. After sizing up the situation, we decided to split our forces since there were two different shoots going on at the same time on this long cypress pond. It was really a beautiful duck habitat. He headed toward the shoot closest to the dam, and I went toward the back of the pond. After getting closer to my shoot, I could tell there were several shooters, and so I was faced with a real problem. There were several of them and only one of me. Then it occurred to me; I would have to surround them! By the time I got parallel to my shooters it was almost dark, but they continued to blast away at the ducks still coming in. A partial moon helped them see and shoot at ducks silhouetted against the sky. I began to wade the beaver sloughs and potholes, and the water was anywhere from chest deep to knee deep. I had to hold my flashlight and pistol up over my head to keep them dry much of the time.

As I got close to the first shooter, I could barely see his image in the near darkness. I could hear about five people talking to each other about how many ducks they had killed and calling out to each other when a potential shot was headed their way. They were having the time of their life with this wood duck slaughter and showing no signs of slowing down.

As I waded closer to the first shooter, I had determined to get as close to him as I could, any way I could, before making myself known. It was a given that they would take a "bush bond"—take to the bush and run like the devil was after them when they saw me. To them the game warden and the devil were about the same thing and they would run equally fast from them both so I only expected to maybe get one of them. I had to outwit them rather than outrun them, so I devised a plan.

I waded slowly so I wouldn't make a sloshing sound as I made my way ever closer to him. About the time he caught sight of me I was about twenty feet away, but he couldn't recognize me as a Ranger. He said, "Who are you?" I quickly put my finger in front of my lips and made a shhhhhhh sound and kept getting closer to him. Again, he demanded in a loud whisper, "Who are you?" And again I made a shhhhhhh sound and kept walking closer. By the time I got close enough to lay hands on him, I whispered to him as I grabbed his jacket sleeve, "I'm the game warden, give me your gun and ducks. Don't say a word or I'll charge you with interference. Do you understand?" Then he replied in a whisper, "Yes, sir" with an audible gulp.

"Now, tell me who that is over there" as I pointed in the direction of the next closest shooter, and he said, "That's Ted." I said, "Call Ted over here and tell him to bring his gun and ducks with him." To my surprise, he complied perfectly. When Ted asked him why, he adlibbed and said, "Just do as I say." Ted said O.K. and was on his way toward us. While I waited on Ted, I checked my newfound friend's shotgun to see if it was plugged. It wasn't. I had a flashlight but I dare not turn it on just yet.

When Ted arrived, I stood a little behind my new friend, Joey, and stepped out at the last second laying hands on Ted and identifying myself as the game warden. Ted didn't say a word but complied with my commands as Joey had. I asked Ted who that was just beyond where he had been standing, and he told me his name was Bill. I said, "Call him and tell him to come over here and bring his gun and ducks with him." I couldn't believe it when Ted began to call Bill and give him the instructions I had given him. Just like Ted had done, here came good old Bill.

By the time Bill had arrived Joey, Ted, and I had become good buddies and they were just overtaken with the fact that "they had been caught by the man." They both acted a little giddy at the time and became more willing to play along with my little game. When Bill arrived he got the same shock treatment and field check like the others. Then I had Bill calling old John over to where we were. But, John smelled a rat and wouldn't come too close to the crowd. I asked one of them how they had come into this pond. The way I had come was rough, and I didn't want to go back that way with four prisoners. One of them said, "Here is the trail over here and we're parked just in the edge of those woods." So, with their identifications in my possession, we made our way to their vehicles with them carrying the ducks and empty guns.

When we got to their trucks, I asked Bill to call John once more; to my surprise, he came to the trucks and I checked him there. I instructed them to drive down to the pond dam where my corporal had been left and I would be along directly. They even gave me a ride to my car, and in no time the corporal and I were writing several duck violations on these young men. They all seemed to be enjoying the fact that they were caught. I really think it was the bold way in which they had been caught that got their goats so bad. But, they seemed to be enjoying the moment. That thrill ended in the courtroom when they learned what their fines would be.

The corporal had caught three hunters himself, so we had a lot of paperwork to do. There were several violations including no waterfowl stamp, unplugged guns, no licenses, over the limit, and of course hunting ducks after legal hours. Early the next morning when we had enough daylight to see, we went back to the pond and found several more ducks that had not been found the evening before due to the darkness. We made sure the judge was made aware of this count even though we didn't add them to their evening count.

I ran into one of the hunters several months later, and he told me that he would never violate another game and fish law as long as he lived and that he had learned his lesson. It may be pride on my part, but I do love to catch violators by outwitting them. That takes the brag out of them later.

- Chapter 17-
Night of the Night Hunters

One thing I have learned about law enforcement through the years is that where there is strict enforcement of the law, you will have more compliance by the citizens. But when there is little or no enforcement of the laws of the land, lawlessness ensues. The law enforcement officer is the first step in the long process of the criminal justice system. The courts can't do anything with lawbreakers if there are no arrests made. This would be a sorry world if it weren't for law enforcement officers and the law. Both criminal and civil laws are enacted as a rule and guide for a civilized society, and peace-loving people will acknowledge that and comply. The criminal element must be kept in check through strict enforcement. The fear of punishment is a definite deterrent. Well-trained and ethical enforcement officers help to keep their society in check, and voluntary compliance is the result.

Such was not the case in a rural southeast Georgia county back in the early 1980s. The department had recently fired the Ranger of that county for unbecoming and criminal conduct. Times were bad for that county because the sheriff was also suspected of being corrupt, and the whole county had become lawless. There was an epidemic of night deer hunting as illegal and unscrupulous people went out with their spotlights and guns and slaughtered deer throughout the county. Law-abiding citizens were afraid to go out at night.

When the day finally came to elect a new sheriff, the citizens elected an honest man who swore to clean up the county and restore order. One of his campaign promises was to stop the night deer hunting that was going on. The bad guys had been having a heyday, but their time was coming to an end. This sheriff meant business, and one of the first acts of his administration was to launch a campaign to rid the county of these nocturnal vermin.

The sheriff called my boss, the captain, and set up a meeting. The captain and I went down to the sheriff's office of that county and met with the sheriff and his chief deputy, who was his brother. All parties at this meeting were well aware of the problem and we all wanted to put a stop to the illegal activity of that county. We devised a plan to saturate the whole county with enforcement officers and catch as many of these night hunters as we could. The sheriff would get the local media to cover the results of our operation on the front page of the local paper. The captain made arrangements with our pilot in Brunswick to make a night flight on a particular Friday night while the ground units spread out all over the county.

Since the sheriff's department was on a different radio frequency band than we were, we decided to pair up a deputy sheriff with a Ranger in each patrol vehicle. That way, the deputy would know the county and the Ranger could be in contact with the aircraft overhead and would make the Game and Fish charges applicable. The sheriff wanted us to be in position just after dark and remain so until daybreak. There had been some night hunting taking place in the wee morning hours. Since the aircraft could only fly four hours, it was decided that the best time for it to fly would be from 10:00 P.M. until 2:00 A.M. Then, the pilot would break off and head back to Brunswick. Radio silence was the order unless we had something going on. No idle chitchat would be allowed.

With our plans made, we all met at the sheriff's jail facility for a big supper, compliments of the sheriff's department, prior to our long night's work. The sheriff was a gracious host, but he was dead serious about putting a stop to this night hunting in his county. They had a chef preparing steaks for everybody, and after we all had a fine supper we paired off and went to our pre-assigned locations. The sheriff and the captain paired off, the chief deputy and I paired of, and everybody picked a partner. This was one of the best-planned details I had ever been on and would surely produce results. We were ready. Each unit slipped out and went to their assigned position quietly.

We hadn't been in position very long when the first night hunters had made their move. One of our enforcement teams had pulled behind the suspects and when they turned on their blue lights, the chase was on. Those guys took off across the county and a high-speed chase was on. They were caught when they slid into a ditch at an intersection. The first bunch was caught. The officers took them to jail, locked them up for the night, and had their vehicle towed in to the sheriff's department impound. The team then quickly returned to its position. Things were hopping already and tensions were high all over the county.

By 9:00 P.M. another of our teams had caught another truck with two occupants and we now had two bunches in custody. This was a Friday night and there was a high school football game in town. We were confident that our business would pick up after the football game was over, and too, the plane would be up by then. We guessed that things should really get hot around midnight, and we weren't wrong.

In the aircraft were the pilot and an observer. The pilot that night was a real veteran of the Aircraft Unit and had been a personal friend of mine for years. Everybody just affectionately called him Barry, although he was a captain. He was just one of the guys and a great pilot. The observer was a wildlife technician who worked on a management area in the county. He was the perfect man for the job. He was a native of the county and knew it well. He also knew the sheriff's department people personally. Our best were on hand for this night, and the bad guys would pay the price before daybreak.

The aircraft really made a big difference. The occupants could see for miles in all directions and once they saw a spotlight, they would begin to check their map and decide which ground unit to bring in to it. The aircraft observer would check his map and get on the radio and call in the ground support. The aircraft gave us a much better chance of catching more bad guys because it multiplied the ability to see much more than a ground unit could see. If you were on the ground and someone was shining a spotlight a quarter of a mile away, you may not be able to see it, but the aircraft would pick it out like a diamond on a piece of black felt. It was a dark night and just perfect for this detail.

The chief deputy and I listened to the radio traffic that night and had a front row seat to a real play-by-play call of the night's events. We were hearing units all over the county, all night long, talking excitedly about jumping night hunters and being involved in high-speed chases. Two of our teams got in high-speed chases and were just flat outrun. Sometimes, no matter how much air and ground support you have, one will get away. We had lost two bunches this night and we were still going. The plane flew until 2:00 A.M. and landed at the local airport. The observer jumped out, got into his truck, and slipped into a position while the pilot headed home. We still had a long way until daybreak.

A long time went by without any activity across the county and we had about concluded that it might be over for the night. After all, it was almost 4:00 A.M. and nothing much had happened since the plane landed. Bill, the chief deputy, told me that he knew a place where we might see somebody night hunt. So, having nothing to lose, we headed that way. I was driving, and the deputy told me to turn left ahead onto a dirt road, cut off my lights, and creep along slowly. I wasn't too keen on driving without lights in a strange county, but he knew it and guided me along the road. I had rolled my window down and stuck my head out so I could at least see the dim edge of the road. Luckily the road was of light-colored sandy loam and the edge of the road dark, so I could at least make out the image of the road's edge by looking out the side window. I was really creeping along when we saw a flash of light in a field right to our left. It was really bright and appeared to be coming out of the field back to the road we were on. The problem was that I didn't know if we had already passed the field road or hadn't reached it yet.

The deputy excitedly told me to back up, that the field road was behind us. So, I backed up as fast as I dared and they came out onto the dirt road in front of us. They hadn't seen us, and we were still in luck. Would they turn toward us or away from us? I was ready to turn my lights on and take them down front to front if necessary, but I had rather stop them from the rear if I could. As it turned out, they turned to their left, which put them in front of us and headed away. I accelerated to catch them, and that was when I discovered that when I had backed up I had backed my right rear tire into the sandy edge and it was spinning in the loose sand.

The bad guys still didn't see or hear us, so I jumped out and ran up to the driver's window, which was rolled down, and yelled for them to stop. As I ran alongside their truck I grabbed through the window for the driver but he ducked toward the middle of the seat and hit the accelerator. As he sped away I hung on to their door for a while but then let go just in the nick of time. I quickly ran back to my car. By now, Bill was yelling for me to hit it while he pushed. He was a big fellow and pushed with all his might as I spun out of the sand and got traction on the solid roadway. I stopped as Bill got in and we sped away after the bad guys with blue lights flashing. Bill was shouting into the radio for the sheriff and the captain to come to us since they were the closest units. He was telling them our location as I drove quickly down the dirt road, following dust and trying to catch up to the night hunters. Bill shouted to me to watch out up ahead for a sharp curve and I slowed down. As I took the curve I noticed a broken utility pole leaning toward the road and the dust suddenly stopped. I knew they had gone off the road along here somewhere, but where? There were thick woods to our right and a cornfield to the left.

I backed up a bit and stopped in the middle of the dirt road. I took my spotlight and scanned the field to see if I could see any sign of them. There, about 50 yards into the field was a truck sitting without any lights on and what looked like smoke or steam rising from it. It was the bad guys! I turned into the cornfield and drove hurriedly toward the truck. As I approached the truck, I could see the driver standing outside the truck as if he was waiting for us to arrive. He made no attempt to run, but was just standing there as if nothing had happened. He was a tall fellow and was wearing overalls and brogans. It was a new model truck, and it was crushed-in just behind the driver's door. It was the truck I had seen back at the field; the same one that I had hung onto as he sped down the road. I recognized the driver too.

As we approached the truck, the deputy and I got out and came up to the bad guy slowly not knowing if his partner may be in the woods with a bead drawn on us. We were all in the headlights of my car and very vulnerable at this point. I grabbed the guy and put him across the hood of the truck in the spread eagle position. I searched him for weapons and contraband as Bill covered me. We got his identification, cuffed him, put him in the back seat of my car. With him secure, we began to look for the spotlight and gun. One more thing was missing...his partner. I had seen the image of a passenger when I was running alongside the truck earlier. He had taken a "bush bond" with the gun and spotlight. Our second suspect and the evidence we needed for a conviction on night hunting was gone. These guys were sharp. They were not amateurs; they were real pros. They knew that without a gun and light we wouldn't be able to charge them with "hunting deer at night."

In just a few minutes, the sheriff and captain arrived and we got a closer look at that utility pole. That guy had slid into it sideways with his new truck. The truck was only one month old and now it was completely totaled. It could not be driven and the frame was bent in the middle. That rendered it a total wreck. The utility pole was almost broken in half. It was suspended above the ground with the aid of the wires attached to it. A wrecker was called, and that new Chevy truck was towed to the sheriff's impound yard.

That one was the seventh group of night hunters that we had jumped on that night, and five of the seven were apprehended and jailed. After the capture that Bill and I were involved in, there was no more activity that night. As day broke we all gathered back at the sheriff's compound and a most welcome breakfast was prepared for us. All the good stuff, high in cholesterol but also high in taste, was served by the chef that morning. Coffee never tasted so good.

We decided to charge the last guy with "blinding wildlife with lights," "eluding an officer," "speeding," and "resisting arrest." When the day came to take them all to court, we had the backing of the state court judge. The old judge was an elderly fellow who had been made aware of the problem of night hunting in the county and wanted to do his part to put a stop to it. When my defendant was called, he had hired an attorney (who didn't come cheap) and was going to fight the cases against him. He was confident that without a gun and light we wouldn't have a case. After hearing both sides, the judge found the defendant guilty on all charges and proceeded to fine him the maximum fine allowable by law on all charges. When you consider the brand new truck wrecked, the lawyer fees, and the high fines, he paid a great price for night hunting that night, even though he wasn't charged with night deer hunting. Surely his truck insurance premiums would go up.

The local newspaper ran the night's efforts as the headline story and the new sheriff and his department started out with a good reputation of getting the bad guys caught. The night's efforts were very successful. There was an immediate change made in that county's lawlessness. The county enjoyed several years of good law and order thanks to the new sheriff and his partners, the Rangers.

- Chapter 18-
In My Mind I Saw a Deer

Without a doubt, one of the most gruesome duties for a Ranger is working a hunting accident in which someone has been killed or severely injured by gunshot. Over the years I have worked several really bad ones. They are all bad, but some stand out in my memory as the worst.

When the Hunter Safety Law was passed in 1979, the hunter safety course was made mandatory for everyone born on or after January 1, 1961. Up until that time, we made courses available on a volunteer basis and did indeed certify hundreds of students across the state. It has been my pleasure to be involved with the Hunter Education Program in Georgia even before being mandated by Georgia law. I have wondered over the years just how many lives have been saved because of hunter safety courses, but that is impossible to measure. After all, you can't measure what didn't happen, so we must trust that multitudes of hunters have been made safer and have changed their unsafe and unethical behavior.

There is one accident that stands out in my mind as the worst I've ever worked. It involved two brothers. The oldest was 17 and his younger brother had just turned 15. They were hunting on their grandparents' farm out in the country one afternoon. The season was well underway and buck fever was at a fever pitch (no pun intended) as hunters from all over were taking to the woods in an attempt to bag that ever-elusive trophy buck.

That's always the primary thought in the mind of most hunters. They want to get a shot at a monster buck. To bag a trophy is the ultimate challenge for deer hunters across the land, and these two brothers were no exception. They rushed out to grandpa's house after school and hurriedly went to their tree stands without even stopping to put on their fluorescent orange vests. After all, they thought, this is private property and no one will be back here except us.

The 17-year old got into a stand that was built in a big oak tree at the edge of a soybean field, and his younger brother went across the field and into the woods on the other side of the big field. The older brother told me that he could see his brother's white tennis shoes from where he was sitting in his stand and knew where he was all the time. It started to get darker as evening set in. When hunting hours were over, they should have started out of the woods and fields and headed back to the house. But, as most folks will do, they extended their luck and the hunting hours. Just a few more minutes, they thought. Maybe that big buck will step out into the edge of the field now that darkness was settling in and they might get that once in a lifetime shot.

The problem with staying too late is that your eyes and mind begin to play tricks on you and you can't distinguish one thing from another in the near darkness. It has always been my contention that if you can't tell the difference between a buck and a doe, you are staying too late. Both these boys were doing just that. They should have already come down out of their tree stands and headed back home, but they stayed.

Then, the 15-year old climbed slowly down out of his stand and began walking back toward grandpa's house. When he got to the edge of the field, he began to jog across it. It was cold and he hadn't brought a jacket. He was in a hurry to get back to the house where there would be a warm fire and a good supper made by grandma.

Meanwhile, his older brother, still in his stand, saw something coming across the field and raised his rifle to his shoulder. The field dropped off gently toward the woods where the younger brother had been. As the older brother looked through his rifle's scope, he couldn't quite make out what he was looking at. He later told me as I interviewed him, "In my mind, I saw a deer." Those words have haunted my memory over the years: "In my mind I saw a deer." How many youngsters have I warned in hunter safety courses not to let their mind draw a false picture of what they want to see? "In my mind"--those words still echo in the halls of my memory as I have wondered over the years how they have tortured that young man.

Think how horrible it must be for him. He had pulled the trigger and the bullet had gone out the barrel and found its mark in the side of the head of his 15-year-old brother, whose life suddenly ended. He will live no more. He will never have the privilege of finishing school and going to college. He will never know what it will be like to take his favorite girl to the Junior-Senior Prom. He will never marry and have children of his own and know the joy of being a father. He will not enjoy any more life than he had lived up to that fatal afternoon. The older brother could not go back in time and do it all over again, although he had wished it a thousand times. He couldn't make the bullet go back into the barrel and give him a second chance to do the right thing. He had learned the lesson of being sure of your target before you pull the trigger. He had learned it well, but he had learned it too late. How tragic!

I arrived at the field that evening before the ambulance did. The boy's body was lying there in the soybean field. His brain was lying about two feet away from his head. There was blood...much blood. The skin of the face was drawn and looked like a miniature mask, not a human being. The top of his head was gone. It was the most grotesque thing I had ever seen. I knew the older brother had seen the same thing just before running to the house to tell his grandpa that he had just shot his brother. No doubt he had said, "Quick, call an ambulance!" although in his heart he knew it was too late for an ambulance. No doctor, nurse, or emergency room staff could put the life back into his kid brother. He was gone.

It was at the funeral that the 17-year old broke down. As they lowered the casket into the grave, he fell to the ground weeping and crying out for his brother. He was calling his name, but his brother would never answer. He was gone. How final death is. He was gone.

- Chapter 19-
The Flood of '94

As a young child I was taught that the rainbow was a sign of the covenant that the earth would not be destroyed by flood again. Well, we were beginning to wonder in 1994 when a tropical storm stalled over the state of Georgia and brought about the worst flood in the state's recorded history. It was called the worst natural disaster ever to strike the state of Georgia. It left much of central and south Georgia under water.

The worst places hit were Macon, Albany, and literally hundreds of towns and cities between them. The destruction went all the way to the Gulf of Mexico. In Americus, 21 inches of rain fell in just 24 hours. That's nearly two feet of rainfall in a day! The rivers and creeks couldn't take the tremendous amounts of water that nature was pushing through them, and many dams broke as a consequence.

Tropical Storm Alberto had formed in the Gulf of Mexico and in early July 1994 it had moved into Georgia and stalled over the state, flooding the Flint River, the Ocmulgee River, and countless smaller streams. Towns and communities began to lose power, water, and telephone service and quickly became cut off. The whole business district of Montezuma was under water. The city of Albany was cut in two by the Flint River as it rose high above the all-time high flood stage and completely engulfed much of the city. This was a flood like the state of Georgia had never seen. The raging Ocmulgee River flooded many streets in Macon as it rushed out of the banks and across the city flooding homes, businesses, highways and bridges. Interstate 16 was cut off in Macon, and Interstate 75 was cut off in Albany. Travel across the state was almost impossible and completely impossible in some areas.

On July 6 Governor Zell Miller declared a state of emergency, and the Georgia Emergency Management Agency (GEMA) called the Department of Natural Resources (DNR) to respond to the catastrophes in Macon, Montezuma, and Oglethorpe. Sumter and Crisp counties became hard hit, and Rangers of the DNR were called into those areas as well. There was not a state agency that was not being utilized in some way or another. Commissioner Joe Tanner of the Department of Natural Resources said, "We have no higher priority," as he ordered more and more Rangers and technicians into the areas that were hardest hit by the flood. People were cut off in their residences without a way of escape. Rangers with their boats were lifesavers for many hundreds of people who were trapped in their homes and businesses in southwest Georgia.

Statewide, Rangers responded with boats, ATVs, and four-wheel drive trucks. The state patrol was blocking many roads and highways, but the Rangers were proving to be just the thing needed for this emergency situation. In Albany, Rangers were evacuating people by boat and helicopter. The only way to get from the east side to the west side of the city was by helicopter. No boat could survive in the raging Flint River as it roared through Albany on its way to Newton and Bainbridge. Bridges that were still standing literally moaned and vibrated as the torrents raged through them. The waters of death made an eerie sound as they roared through the cities and towns. Separate headquarters were set up on the east and west sides of Albany. The west side had power for the most part, as did most of the motels, restaurants, and business district. The east side was without power and was made up primarily of residential sections.

In many cases, people refused to leave their belongings. It was chaotic, with people calling for help as the swift, rising water cut off thousands of people from evacuation. The DNR helicopter shuttled people and supplies to and from areas that were cut off. Below Albany, the towns of Newton and Bainbridge became cut off with no way out.

Just when you think things can't get worse, you find out different. We heard that the dam on Lake Blackshear broke upstream from us. Lake Blackshear is a reservoir on the Flint River. When the word came that the dam had broken, there were several people who got in their vehicles and headed east, away from Albany. We found out that the water level below the dam was about the same as above the dam, so the dam breaking was of little consequence. It wasn't going to make a surge of floodwater in Albany as some thought. That just meant that the floodwaters would not subside as soon as we had hoped. The flood was taking a toll everywhere.

Churches responded with hundreds of bag meals and drinking water for rescued people and rescuers alike. Food and water became a high priority for everyone in the flood areas. Tap water was toxic as it became contaminated by the floodwaters. Sewerage systems were overwhelmed and raw sewage was swept into the raging torrents. Now, it was dangerous in more ways than one. A local brewery using their canning facilities, canned drinking water in specially prepared cans. This emergency supply of water was much needed and a wonderful gesture on their part. It was amazing how people were all doing their part to help their fellow man.

Some 250 DNR personnel responded to Albany with 175 boats. Not only were hundreds of people rescued, our Rangers also rescued stranded pets that had taken refuge on rooftops, porches, trees, or anywhere they could find footing. They were scared, tired, and hungry like everybody else.

As waters receded, activity went from a water operation to a land operation. There, too, Rangers responded with their ATVs (all-terrain vehicles). ATVs became a priority to prevent looting. Rangers patrolled in pairs and guarded business and residential sections that had been flooded. Before the people could return, the Rangers had to patrol the areas to keep unauthorized people out.

But the worst of the flood wasn't realized until the waters receded and we were able to discover that caskets had floated out of their places in the cemeteries. There were scores of caskets that had floated out of saturated and flooded ground and had drifted into trees, fences and anything that halted their drifting. This cleanup became one of the most heart-rending details of the entire flood disaster. The governor had ordered the Georgia Bureau of Investigation to the area to help identify the bodies and return them to their respective burial sites and re-inter them. The Department of Natural Resources partnered with the GBI to accomplish this important duty. All DNR personnel who worked on this detail were volunteers. Not one Ranger was assigned against their will. It was a hazardous but necessary operation and the Rangers and special agents who responded did so with the dignity of professionals, responding to the loved ones of the city's residents.

During the flood, I was assigned to the east side of Albany as the night shift supervisor. I was in charge of all the Rangers and technicians on that side of the city. I had to provide for their meals and lodging as well as make work assignments. During the first days of the disaster, it was difficult for everybody. Sergeant Lindsey, the day shift supervisor, and I had to set up a command post. We inventoried and secured needed supplies and materials and provided for food and lodging for our troops. Since the governor had declared a state of emergency, we had statewide priority to obtain supplies, material, and additional personnel. We were on 12-hour shifts for the two weeks that we were in Albany.

One night I got on the phone and called a colonel at the Georgia Army National Guard Headquarters in Atlanta and asked him to send me night vision goggles and Humvees. I explained to him that we had areas that were flooded and in some places, it was too shallow for boats and in other places it was too deep for trucks. I also explained that my Rangers needed to see during the night hours to prevent looting and vandalism. He told me that he would see what he could do. The next day he sent a helicopter to Albany with 200 night vision goggles with regrets that he couldn't get any Humvees to me. Those night vision goggles made a world of difference in our effectiveness as we "controlled the night" in Albany.

There was a total nighttime curfew and anyone caught out of doors after 10:00 P.M. was arrested. There were several arrests made by my men for violations of curfew. We confiscated drugs, weapons, and got in some high-speed chases through the blacked-out streets of the east side. It was a different story on the west side of the city. There were busy, well-lit streets with restaurants, coffee shops, shopping malls, and other establishments that had power. On our side of the river there was only one restaurant that had power. Our option for restaurants was limited to that one restaurant. We had to travel more than 50 miles to Moultrie to find motel rooms. That made our 12-hour shift seem longer and the added travel time cut into our much needed sleep time. Sleeping during the day was not a problem for most Rangers since they were used to working night details and sleeping during daylight hours sometimes.

The heat and humidity was another problem that was almost impossible to overcome. The only place where we could find an air conditioner was in a vehicle. We were thankful to be on the night shift since it was a bit cooler at night, but not much. Nights felt like a sauna, and daytime was much worse. The heat and humidity made sleep much more difficult. When you are as tired as we were, you could sleep anywhere. By the end of the two weeks, everybody had the "thousand-yard-stare." We were hollow-eyed, bone-tired, and home-sick. Everybody was ready to get back home and return to his or her usual duties.

The floodwaters slowly receded and the creeks and rivers were finally back in their banks. Hundreds of homes and businesses were totally destroyed. Many more were ruined by water damage. Vehicles, personal property, lives, homes, crops, and livestock were all destroyed or suffering. As the waters receded, our work as rescuers and protec-tors was over. Now we could leave the flooded areas and let the people try to put their lives back together. Return and recovery was the order of the day as officials breathed an exhausted sigh of relief that the worst was finally over. This flood of 1994 was declared to be a "Five Hundred Year" disaster.

The drive home was long and tiring, but much welcomed. It was so good to get home to my wife and children and finally sleep in my own bed.

If anyone ever asks me if I've ever been to Albany, I think I will say, "Yes, I spent two weeks there one night." That was what it felt like, a night that lasted two weeks. I have never worked so hard in all my life before or since. I don't ever want to see a flood again. Noah, you can have the floods. Just show me a rainbow.

- Chapter 20-
City of the Dead

Catching night hunters is a big part of the Ranger's job during the fall and winter months. It always seems that November is the peak month for this sort of activity, so that's about the time of the year when Rangers are really hopping. Long hours and a lot of night work are the order of the day for that time of the year.

There was a time when the deer population was very low or nonexistent and deer were being introduced into the wild once again. They required much protection until we could maintain viable populations. In those early days, night hunters could really do the future deer herd a lot of damage by killing them before they had a chance to get established. Rangers set up night details to bag the bad guys. Once these violators were caught, the courts could deal with them and hand out some very hefty fines in an attempt to stop this illegal and unethical activity.

Over the years, the deer population has grown tremendously in most states, but night deer hunters are still a problem, not so much because of the damage they do to the deer herd as much as being extremely unsafe and unethical. Most night hunters don't care whose land they hunt on or where they find their quarry. Many times deer are found dead from those unscrupulous people who just want to shoot them for the fun of shooting them. They don't intend to make good use of the meat. They just kill to be killing and that, in my opinion, is a waste of the resource, not to mention the unethical nature of it.

There are certain night hunters who make hunting deer at night their career. I really think it is more of a "cat and mouse" game they like to play with the Rangers. I have had the displeasure of knowing many such individuals, but one stands out in my mind as a really notorious one. We knew him by name, and he knew us by name. We all knew what the other was doing. We knew he was killing deer at night, and he knew we were trying to catch him. This guy was building quite a reputation with the locals as a man who couldn't be caught. They said he was just too slick. What a challenge! That's the kind of reputation I like to destroy. The best way to break that junk up is to catch him and catch him quickly. That would kill his reputation and build ours at the same time. I loved it.

This one was really slick. One night as my partner and I were going home after a long night detail, he called me on the radio and asked me to come to his house. I was nearly home, but I turned around and went to his house. I knew he wouldn't have called me if he didn't need me. He said that he had something to show me. When I arrived there at his driveway, he was waiting for me. He had a long driveway and the house was well out of sight of the main highway. When I got out of my truck, he pointed to his mailbox by the road and said, "Look at that, Jim." Someone had hung the head and cape of a freshly killed doe deer over his mailbox. It was about 2:00 A.M., and the blood was still fresh on the cape. Talk about bold. This guy had done this while we were out trying to catch him. He must have laughed his way home and gone to bed thinking he had pulled one over on the Rangers. He probably thought we didn't know who did it.

"You know who did this, don't you, Jim?" he asked. "Yep, it was old Ray," I answered. "I've a good mind to give it back to him right now," he said disgustedly. "Heck, I'm game, partner, if you are," I said. And, we took it off his mailbox and laid it in the bed of his truck and headed down the road toward Ray's house. We knew where Ray lived and which mailbox was his. I was driving, and my partner wanted to be the one who put it on his mailbox. He said he wanted to return the favor. I turned my headlights off about a quarter of a mile before we got to his house. I stopped the truck a few hundred yards short of his house so there would be no vehicle noise. He might still be up, and we didn't want him to catch us giving his little present back. Two can play this game, we thought.

My partner grabbed the bloody thing from the bed of the truck and took off down the road in a trot. In a few minutes, he returned huffing and puffing and said excitedly, "Take off! Let's get out of here." I cranked the truck and eased down the road with lights off for a ways then when we were sure to be clear I turned them on and we went on back to my partner's house. I got my vehicle and headed home with the satisfaction that we had played his game too. Letting him know that we knew was the sweetest part of it. We wanted him and we wanted him badly. He knew it too. Now, he would know for sure.

The next morning my phone rang; it was my partner. "You ain't gonna believe what I found draped across my mailbox early this morning," he said. "You've got to be joking," I exclaimed. "No, I'm not joking, Jim. That SOB put it right back on my mailbox early this morning," he said. Man, this guy was beginning to get on our nerves. I was steaming, and that was mild compared to how my partner felt. We had to get him! This thing had gone too far.

Our sergeant had caught him several years earlier, but he hadn't been caught since. He didn't pay a fine that time because his uncle was the judge of the court that handled his case, and the case just remained there on the docket without being called. They never called it up. The sergeant would be in court every session, waiting for the case to be called but to no avail. This went on for a long time, and then one day when he couldn't be there, they called the case up and promptly dismissed it due to the lack of a prosecuting witness. Talk about crooked justice. That's one reason he was so bold. He knew if he got caught, the case would never come up, which was like never being brought to trial. So far, he was winning this conflict and making us look bad in the process.

This guy was no amateur or novice. He wasn't a kid either. He had just recently retired from the Army and was a seasoned soldier. He put all his training and stealth to work for him, and he was good, real good. The Marine in me couldn't let this guy best me. I had to put my best training to work also. It was going to take a fox to catch a fox. My partner and I began to work tirelessly gathering intelligence on this guy. One of us would lay surveillance on his house to get an idea when he was coming and going and which direction he went when he pulled out of his driveway. He would use his mother's house, too, so the other would lay surveillance on her house also. When we had gathered our intelligence, we devised our plans. We suspected that he would pull around behind old country churches and barns and the like, checking for Rangers or signs of where a Ranger had been set up. If he found nothing, he would shine the fields there, knowing that he had "cleared" the area first. Sometimes he would go into an area that he wanted to hunt and shine a spotlight just to see if he could pull a Ranger out of his hiding place. He would leave his gun at home just in case he was pulled over. If no Ranger came out, he would return a little later with his gun. He was slick indeed.

There was a particular area that he liked to hunt. The problem was, there was no place to hide a truck there. He knew that, and that's why he liked that area so much. He really picked his spots and times well. As you traveled down that particular road, there was a beautiful field on the right in a big long sweeping curve. There was a church on the left side of the road right in the middle of the curve. Usually, behind the church would be the perfect place to hide a truck, but you couldn't get behind this church because of a fence and also there were two yard lights shining brightly. The church was not a good place to wait and watch from. There, next to the church, was a big cemetery. You couldn't hide a truck there either. But wait. Who says you have to hide a truck? I would lay surveillance near the church and watch the field and call my partner on the portable radio if I saw anything. I would be the eyes and ears of the operation, and my partner would be the catch man.

When the time came, I got my partner to drop me off at the church before proceeding to his position about a mile down the road. I had my sleeping bag for warmth, my big thermos bottle of coffee, and my portable radio. I was going to lie in the cemetery behind one of those big headstones. As I walked through the cemetery, my mind began to think spooky thoughts. I thought about all those dead people lying just a few feet below me. Being in the city of the dead was not a thought that I relished. I was actually going to lie on a dead person to catch this bad guy. It was so spooky it just might work. I don't think Ray, the bad guy, would have dreamed that one of us would lie in the cemetery to catch him, but like I said earlier, it takes a fox to catch a fox.

The yard lights in the churchyard threw just enough light across the cemetery to enable me to see my way without a flashlight, but it also cast some really scary shadows through the tombstones. My partner was about a mile down the road, which, incidentally, dead-ended into the lake. The culprit had to come and go by my position, so if he came by me, he was headed toward a dead end. We hoped to trap him like the rat he was. I spread my USMC surplus sleeping bag behind one of the big headstones and got in it. It was a cold night. I was set. Now we would see what happened. We had nothing to lose.

As I lay there, I remembered running into Ray at a little country store at the crossroads near his house about two weeks earlier. I had stopped for a soft drink and he came out the door as I was walking up to it. He was noticeably uncomfortable, running in to me like that. He looked like he just wanted to keep walking by without speaking and get the heck out of there. I couldn't let this opportunity pass by without speaking to him. It gave me a chance to feel him out. I struck up a conversation with him and he obliged, although he was uncomfortable doing so. "Ray, why do you shoot deer at night?" I asked. "You don't need the meat and I don't think you're selling the deer. Why do you do it?" I inquired. "I don't hunt deer at night," he denied. "Aw, come on, Ray," I said, "you and I both know you are hunting deer at night. Really, I just want to know what it is that makes you do it." At that, he paused and stared at me for several seconds. Then he asked, "You really want to know, don't you?" "Yep, I really want to know," I said. Then he turned to me, just as cool as an ice cube, and said, "I just love to watch them sons-a-bitches drop." Then he turned and walked away. What a cool calculating character he was.

It had been at least three hours since my partner had dropped me off at the cemetery. A few cars and trucks came by but they just kept going. Then, about 3:00 A.M., after everything had become very quiet, I saw a vehicle coming down the road slowly. There was no telltale spotlight out the window, no shots fired, just slowly moving until it came to the church driveway. As the truck turned in at the church, the headlights swept across the cemetery. I ducked behind a short wall and lay flat, not making a sound. Almost without thinking, I reached and turned the volume all the way down on the radio. I peeped over the wall in time to see the truck's headlights go off and hear the engine go silent. The driver stepped out of the truck, and as I peered from behind a big headstone, I could see in the glow of the nightlight that it was Ray. My heart was beating so fast I felt sure he could hear it from there. Surely, it was about to jump right out of my chest. I remained motionless and just watched him. For a while he did nothing except stand there and look around. I dared not move, and I couldn't call my partner. If I could, what would I tell him? Ray wasn't doing anything . . .yet!

Then, he ambled slowly over to his truck, got in, cranked it, and drove out the driveway. He didn't turn his headlights on. Then, without warning, out the window came the spotlight and he began to sweep the field across the road from the church. The truck stopped and just sat there with the spotlight sweeping the big field. By now, I had called my partner and put him on alert. "Don't come here just yet, he hasn't shot, but he's shining a light," I explained on the radio. About that time, KABLOOIE!!! I almost jumped out of my skin. "Come on! Come on! Come on! He just shot," I said excitedly. I felt helpless. I couldn't do anything except keep my partner posted on his movements. Ray must have either missed the deer or he intended to come back later and retrieve it because he just drove off.

He headed down the road in the direction of my partner and out of my sight. I began to run in that direction and as I got to the road, I could see the headlights of my partner's truck coming. I watched as he pulled Ray over with blue lights flashing. They were about a half-mile away from where I was. Boy, did I ever want to be there. I kept running, wondering all the time what was going on. Was Ray giving my partner a hard time? Was my partner accomplishing the arrest without any trouble? I had left the portable radio at the cemetery because it was so heavy and bulky. In no time I arrived on the scene huffing and puffing, out of breath but still feeling like a million bucks. We had caught Mr. Smart Guy! What a score! My partner already had him handcuffed by the time I got there and was strutting like a peacock. Ray was visibly shaken. When I got there, Ray asked me, "Where did you come from?" I was glad he asked. I told him where I had been lying and what I had seen. "You've been caught, big boy," I gloated, "and this time you're not going to get off."

I drove Ray's truck and followed my partner to the sheriff's department jail facility, where we booked Ray. We filled out all the paperwork to condemn his vehicle and firearm. We didn't get in a hurry either. We took our sweet time while Ray sat in jail. We didn't know how long he would stay in there, but we knew he would be there as long as we were there.

This is not the end of this story. I'm happy to say that before a month had gone by, my partner had caught him again. That's right! He now had two pending charges of night deer hunting against him. Our captain went with us to talk to the prosecuting attorney. We insisted that this time he come quickly before a judge, and it had better not be his uncle. We actually asked for a change in venue, but he assured us that it wasn't necessary. This was a new solicitor and not the same one our sergeant had dealt with. We got convictions on both cases we had against him. He paid several hundred dollars in fines and lost two different vehicles and guns through civil condemnation. Back then Georgia law provided for the filing of civil action to seize and confiscate any vehicles and firearms used in the commission of hunting deer at night. He who laughs last laughs best. Now Ray had the reputation of having been caught not once but three times by the Rangers. Our reputations grew in that county also, and we didn't mind.

The last I heard of Ray, he was turning out to be a really decent guy. He may not have been a model citizen, but he seemed to be walking the straight and narrow now.

- Chapter 21-
The Germans

Answering complaint calls is a big part of a Ranger's job. I received a complaint call one day by phone from a man who had a strong German accent. I went to his home on Dozier Road to see what his problem was. On the phone he had said something about people shooting at his deer from the road.

When I arrived at his house, a large Great Dane greeted me. As I pulled into the driveway, this dog came up to my car barking and was so tall he was looking right into my window at me, face to face. What a dog! I believe you could put a saddle on this canine and take a ride. I wasn't about to step out of the car with this thing barking at me. Fortunately, the man came out the door and called the dog off. The protective monster obeyed his master, and the man invited me to get out. "He wan bite you; hees djus a big beeby," he said in his heavy German accent. Trusting his assessment, I slowly got out of the car. I had never been sniffed by anything bigger than me, but this big dog gave me the once-over and returned to his couch.

The man was tall, in his mid-forties, and had a beautiful little farm. He pointed to a small bottomland pasture in the curve of the road down the hill from the house. He said that was where the deer came out in the afternoon to graze. Apparently, someone had been riding by and taking shots at them as they fed. There was a little red barn beside his driveway that was just perfect for me to hide my car behind and watch the area without being seen from the road. I planned to sit there for a few late afternoons and see if I could catch someone shooting at the deer.

I returned to the home late that afternoon and planned to work it until nearly dark. As I carefully backed my car around behind the little red barn, I could see the man come out of the house and walk my way. Once in position, I got out of the car and we sat on the hood and talked. He was a most interesting fellow to talk with, and I appreciated the company. These surveillance details can get long and boring sometimes. As with most details like this, you may sit for hours with nothing happening and all of a sudden things happen quickly. Excitement may be minutes away, so you have to be patient.

Life is full of little surprises, and this day was about to present one to me. As I sat talking with this gentleman, I heard his wife come out the back door and begin to call a pet. I thought she was calling that saddle-dog but I could see her walk from the house toward the woods that lay just a few yards beyond their lawn. She was calling, "Here, biddy, biddy, biddy; here, biddy, biddy, biddy." As soon as her husband heard this, he told me to come see this. "Vee vait here until she gets him to come, zen ve go see," he said. I just watched to see what they were talking about, and then out of the late evening woods stepped a half-grown doe deer. It came out of the woods and trotted right up to her. She was holding a baby bottle in her hand, and the deer walked right up to her and began to suck the bottle. As it sucked, she walked backward through the open sliding glass door and into the house. Both woman and deer went right into the kitchen. Her husband then turned to me and said, "It's O.K. now, ve go insidt." I just followed him right into the house. There was his wife backed against the kitchen counter for support as this half-grown deer sucked the bottle. It bumped and pushed at the bottle as it sucked. If I hadn't seen it I wouldn't have believed it.

A deer living out in the woods comes to the house when called and makes itself at home, inside the house.

This was obviously no completely wild deer. The couple showed me a wound down the deer's back that they said was where an arrow had gone just under the skin along the backbone. They had removed the arrow and nursed the deer back to health. The hair on its spine was missing from its shoulders to its tail, but the deer was in very good health and was healing just fine. As she fed the animal, we stroked it with our hands just as you would pet a dog. After it finished the bottle, it went out the door and back into the woods.

I'll be doggone if that wasn't the strangest thing I'd ever seen. It was obvious to me they weren't trying to keep a pet since they had turned it back into the wild. They told me that it was getting harder and harder to get it out of the woods and one day it would just not come when called. That was the right thing to do. It is always best to transition wildlife back into the wild, and they were doing just that. After all, the place for wildlife is in the wild, and they had turned it back where it belonged. I guess they just gave an injured creature a helping hand and had made a friend in the process. It was obvious that the deer appreciated their help, but the day was coming when it would stay with its own kind and forget the helping hand.

As for the road hunters shooting at the deer in the bottom pasture, they were caught the next afternoon. I was in my hiding place behind the red barn when a truck came along and slowed as it approached the curve where the deer were standing in the pasture. Kaboom! A shot was fired and I jumped in my car and took off out the driveway and sped toward them. When they heard me coming, they pulled off quickly but my big Ford was just too much car for them, and they were caught. With blue lights flashing, I approached the truck. There were two guys inside the truck and about three guys riding in the bed of the truck. They all had guns. I collected their licenses and identification and saw that they were all local men.

As I checked their guns, one of them had an old single-barrel shotgun and I saw something I had never seen. He had taken a pocketknife and cut a crimp around the middle of the shell. The ring was cut around a 12-gauge # 7 shot shell. What he had done was an attempt to make a slug shell out of a # 7 shot shell by cutting the shell casing almost in two. That was a dumb idea because that half of the shell casing would probably hang in the barrel of the gun when it was fired. That would cause an obstruction in the barrel and would, in all probability, blow up in the guy's face the next time he fired the gun. Dumb!

They all received tickets that day for "hunting from a public road" and "hunting from a motor vehicle." I could have charged them with "hunting on lands of another without permission," but I didn't want to load them down with citations. They got the message, and this bunch wouldn't bother the deer anymore. The Germans were happy that I had caught the culprits, and I had another strange story to add to my memoirs. Life goes on with still another example of truth being stranger than fiction.

- Chapter 22-
The Preacher and the Polygraph

It was a very cold January night that we had picked to set up a detail to catch night deer hunters. This was a concentrated patrol involving several Rangers scattered across most of a south-central Georgia county. The Ranger assigned to the county that we were working, had done his homework and had picked out the positions for each Ranger to watch. Apparently, there was a problem with people hunting deer at night by foot. Most night hunters would ride the roads and shine a spotlight out the window into a field or pasture where they thought deer would be standing. If they saw deer, they would shoot the deer, load it into their truck and speed away before anyone could call a Ranger to respond. Usually by the time a Ranger arrived, the perpetrator was long gone with the meat. But, these guys were hunting by walking the fields and woods, especially on moonlit nights, and shooting deer. They usually had a pickup man who would meet them at a certain place to pick up them and their deer.

On that cold January night I was sitting behind an old abandoned farmhouse that was now being used as a hay storage barn. It was set up in a good spot because it was located about a hundred yards off the main highway with pastures on both sides. I had another Ranger sitting with me that night. This was such a remote part of the county that passing vehicles were scarce. That made the time pass much slower.

It was about 3:00 A.M. when we were sitting there in my patrol car drinking coffee and talking to pass the time. Then, all of a sudden we saw a bright sweeping light and it startled us both. There hadn't been a vehicle by in a long time, so where did the light come from? About the time we were trying to determine its location, we heard three loud shots. They were too close together to be one shooter. There must be at least two of them, and they were shooting deer close to us. Very close!

My partner jumped out of the car in an attempt to hear better and see if he could see anyone. The pasture beside the old abandoned house went uphill toward the road from where we were sitting. We couldn't actually see the highway from where we were sitting but could see a vehicle passing by. Instinctively, I cranked the car and pulled up to the road to see if we could see any vehicles on the highway. I hadn't turned on my lights and I had my blackout switches turned off. Blackout switches are usually toggle switches that are installed on a Ranger's vehicle that when turned off will keep your brake lights, tail lights, and back-up lights from coming on. You could then be totally blacked out in the darkness; and except for the engine noise, no one would know you were there. It was most effective.

In no time we were at the road. Then, to our right there was a flashlight flicker just down the road and over the fence into the pasture. We rolled slowly down the road toward the light, and my partner was ready. He had his window down so he could see and hear better and was ready to pounce! As we got almost adjacent to where we had seen the light, my partner jumped out and quickly climbed the fence and hit the ground running on the other side. As he jumped the fence and hit the ground, he turned on his flashlight and yelled, "Halt, game warden!" He was in hot foot pursuit of someone whom I never saw. I jumped out of the car and over the fence to help him give chase. By the time I got into the middle of the pasture, my partner was coming back in my direction, out of breath. "I'm not sure but I think there were two of them," he said while huffing and puffing. "Man, could those guys run," he exclaimed. "They just flat out ran me," he admitted.

When we returned to the road where my car was parked, we found two high-powered rifles and a doe deer next to the fence. They had shot a deer and had pulled it up to the fence as if they were to be picked up there. They had left their guns propped against the fence and the deer next to them. We began to look for footprints in the pasture and found the guy's tracks where my partner had chased him. Judging by the distance between his tracks, he must have been a long-legged fellow. He was just hitting a spot here and there. He had done some long-stride running and had just outrun my short-legged partner. While we were tracking him, we found a toboggan cap lying there that the guy had apparently run right out from under. He was running so fast he had lost his toboggan. As I picked up this knit cap, I shined my flashlight into the cap and I could see several sandy blonde hairs in the fabric. I kept that toboggan and the rifles for later evidence and identification. It's amazing what the crime lab could do with hair, firearms, and fingerprints.

After riding up and down the road a few times and seeing nothing, we decided to return to our hiding spot and see if a pickup man came by. Sure enough, about ten minutes later a car came down the road at a normal rate of speed until it reached our area. As it approached where we were, it slowed to within about 15 miles per hour and passed by slowly. As the vehicle passed by, we heard the horn beep two short, distinctive beeps and then passed on. In a couple of minutes, it returned the same way and went through the same routine. It slowed down, gave two distinctive beeps, and moved on. It didn't completely stop but passed so slowly it wouldn't be hard to trot up to it if you wanted to.

After about the third pass we decided we would pull him over. We watched him as he slowed, beeped his horn, and moved on down the highway. I cranked my car, pulled up to the roadway, and drove toward him for about two hundred yards before I turned my headlights on and caught up to him. By then he was a quarter of a mile or more away from the place where he had been beeping. If the bad guys were watching, we didn't want them to see or hear us.

After catching up to the questionable vehicle on the highway, I turned on the blue lights and stopped him. He was a white male about 35 years old and was noticeably nervous and shaking. After we got his identification, I read him his Miranda Warning and began to ask him questions about the identity of those guys that he was trying to pick up. "I don't know what you are talking about," he said. He kept denying that he was involved in any night deer hunting. He adamantly proclaimed his innocence and flatly denied that he knew anything about any night hunters. If I hadn't seen what he did with my own eyes, I would have been prone to believe him. He was most believable. But the problem was, I knew he was telling a lie.

Then, my partner came up with an idea. "Jim, let's use his car to see if we can get them to come out to us," he said. "Hey, that's a great idea," I said. We parked and locked my car and got into his car. I drove and my partner sat by the passenger's door. We put the suspect between us in the front seat and we started driving by the area where the deer and rifles had been left. As we came up to the area we did just like he had done; we slowed down and beeped the horn twice, just like he had been doing.

On the second pass of trying this, we got lucky. Two guys jumped across the fence and quickly ran up to the car as if they were going to jump in. But just before they grabbed the handle, one shined a flashlight through the window and right into my partner's face. I can't tell you how fast those guys got out of there. When they hit the fence, it sounded like someone tuning a five-stringed banjo. Twang! My partner gave the second chase of the night but with the same results. At least, now we knew the guy we had in custody was the pickup man. Off to jail we went with the bird in the hand. But there were two in the bush!

When we got to the county jail, we made out all our charges and did all the necessary paperwork. While we were booking the man, he told us he was a preacher. "Preacher, why are you out here in the wee hours of the morning with these other men killing deer?" asked the jailer. He responded that he was not a night hunter and didn't even own a gun. Well, you don't have to own a gun to be involved in illegal activity. Driving the pickup car was at least aiding and abetting night deer hunters. At any rate, he went into the pokey that night. Morning was just a couple of hours away, and the sheriff would be in soon. I wondered how he would respond to us locking up a preacher.

After we finished our booking procedure, we went back to the scene where other Rangers had gathered and were combing the woods and trying to find the two who ran. It was one of the coldest nights of the year, and I knew these guys were probably extremely cold, especially if they had gotten wet in the creek below the pasture. We searched the rest of the night with no results, so as day was breaking we went home for a few hours of much needed sleep.

By noon the sheriff's office had called my house and informed me that the sheriff wanted to meet with us. I called my partner and arranged to pick him up, and we went to meet the sheriff and the defendant. When we arrived, we greeted the sheriff, shook hands, and immediately got down to business. The sheriff wanted to know if we had seen the preacher shine a light, or shoot at a deer. I could tell that he had a strong inclination to believe the preacher and discount us. He was about to turn the preacher loose, and I knew it. I then told the sheriff every detail about how he had slowed down, blown his horn twice, and repeated this several times. I told him that when we did the same thing that the preacher had done, the suspects came running to us and almost jumped in the car with us. "Sheriff, they knew that car, and I'm sure they knew this man, and he knows who they are," I said sternly. "Sheriff, he might be a preacher, but he's guilty. He's not the first preacher I've caught night deer hunting," I said. "He might be guilty, but I'm going to release him on his own recognizance," he said. "I have no problem with that, sir. It's just that I think we can get him to talk to those other two boys and get them to give themselves up," I explained.

I told the preacher that we had a lot of physical evidence that we would use to find these guys. I told him that we would get the Federal Alcohol, Tobacco, and Firearms Agency to run the guns and trace them to the last owners. I told him that we had already lifted finger-prints from the guns and that the toboggan had several hair samples in it. I told him that all these items were being sent to the Georgia Crime Lab in Savannah. "Preacher, if you want to help those boys, talk them into giving themselves up to us," I said. "It will go a lot easier on them than if we have to use investigative means to find them. The judge will probably give them some time on this one," I told him. I really wanted him to get those boys to come in and give themselves up. That would be a lot easier on everybody.

The preacher didn't say he would do as I suggested, because that would hurt his case because of his statement that he was inno-cent. If he agreed to talk to the other two suspects, it would be an admission that he knew them and would thereby blow his case. The sheriff allowed him to go free but told him that he was to return to court when he was summoned. I made sure I had his home phone number so I could continue to stay in touch with him. I didn't want this case to grow cold.

The next day I got another call from the sheriff. He asked that my partner and I come to his home and meet with him and the preacher-defendant. It surprised me that he wanted everybody to meet at his home. He wanted us to have an informal fact-finding meeting so we could clear this case without taking it to trial. That suited me but I doubted that the preacher would budge from his story. The defendant and the sheriff had met and talked before we arrived and that by their design. I think the sheriff wanted to see if he and the defendant could work it out before we arrived, but that didn't happen.

When we arrived, everybody sat down in the sheriff's den. He was a hospitable and gracious host. I'll have to admit that it did create a more relaxed atmosphere. I think the sheriff wanted to get to the truth in an unofficial way and spare the preacher public embarrassment. As we talked, the defendant stuck with his story as solidly as ever, and we were getting nowhere fast. Then the sheriff looked at us all and said, "I know how to resolve this thing. We'll all get in my car and go to the GBI office in Douglas and have the preacher take a polygraph." When he said that, the defendant looked pale but agreed reluctantly. Then the sheriff turned to the preacher and said, "If you're telling me the truth, that thing will tell us, and I'll turn you loose right on the spot and tear these game wardens' case tickets up." The preacher looked really pale when the sheriff said that. One thing that I have picked up over the years of dealing with people is to read their reactions and get a feel of whether they are telling the truth or a lie. It's not foolproof, but it worked for me on most occasions. I could tell that he was shaken, so I moved in really close to him and got face to face and said, "Preacher, I can't look into your heart and tell if you're telling the truth or not; only the Lord could do that. But this polygraph is the closest thing we have to being able to look into a person's heart and tell whether they are telling the truth or a lie."

That little bombshell must have hit him hard in the right place. After I said that, we all headed toward the door to go to Douglas. He knew we weren't running a bluff and that we were really going to hook him up to the polygraph. Then, as we all reached the door, he turned to the sheriff and said, "No, there isn't any use in going to Douglas. I did it. I am guilty just like the Rangers said. I was going to pick up those boys that night just like they claim."

Now business was picking up and we sat back down. He began to tell the sheriff and us everything that happened that night. He filled in a lot of gaps in our case and confessed to everything, but he would not name the other two defendants. He promised us that he would talk to them both and see if he could get them to come in and give themselves up to us. The sheriff commended him for coming clean and promised to keep this from going to court. I wholeheartedly agreed that we would serve no useful purpose in dragging this thing through the courts when it could be handled with a simple bond forfeiture. There was nothing to be gained by conducting a character assassination on this man. All we wanted was justice.

The next morning, the preacher called me and told me that he had gotten one of the boys to agree to come in and give himself up, but the other one wouldn't come in. I called the sheriff and told him about that, and he met us there. As the preacher, the sheriff, and I waited for the mysterious defendant to arrive, we just chatted. I got to know the preacher much better. As we talked and got better acquainted, in walked a tall, lanky, sandy blonde young man who looked to be about 6' 4" or taller. He came through the door and introduced himself to me. He was the one with the long stride and the toboggan. After I got his written statement of the night in question, I wrote his citations and gave them to the sheriff. The two were allowed to post a cash bond and then forfeit the bond in lieu of appearing in court.

The third man remained unknown and neither of the other defendants would give his name. They both said that he had learned his lesson and was scared to death. I guess two in the hand was better than two in the bush, so we agreed not to pursue the third defendant at the insistence of the other two. There was an apparent hardship that they wouldn't tell us about. I honored their request and the case was closed.

The preacher and I became good friends and have remained so through the years. We have visited each other's church and had lunch together on several occasions when I would be in his area. He is a good fellow who just got mixed up in something he shouldn't have, but I don't hold that against him. All in all, I think we won on all sides with this case. We stopped the night hunting by foot, the local Ranger was very pleased, the county sheriff had a new respect for the Rangers, we saved the reputation of a minister, and I had made a new friend. That's not bad for a night's work.

- Chapter 23-
Tulsa or Die

There is a wonderful organization known as The Southeastern Association of Fish and Wildlife Agencies of which Georgia is a member. The "Southeastern," as it is affectionately called, is a division of The International Association of Fish and Wildlife Agencies. It is an organization of sister states in the southeastern United States that share many common problems and solutions. Each member state benefits from its association with the other member states.

Each year there is a competition of technical papers that is conducted among the several sections of wildlife issues. In other words, there is a competition among the Fisheries Sections of the several states, the Game Management Sections, the Law Enforcement Sections, the Hunter Education/Outdoor Education Section, and so forth. Members from each state's agency section can submit a paper for the competition in the Southeastern. It is quite an honor just to be chosen by your state to represent it by submitting your paper into the competition.

It was my distinct honor to submit a paper entitled "Law Enforcement Ethics and Professionalism" into the competition in the state of Georgia. To my complete surprise, my paper was chosen as the top paper in the Georgia competition. Now I would be going to the annual convention of the Southeastern to present my paper. The convention that particular year was to be held in Tulsa, Oklahoma. I could hardly wait to present my paper. I was on pins and needles with excitement.

There were events that led up to my choosing a topic for my paper. My department and the state patrol had both been recently embarrassed by two of its officers who had been caught escorting

drug shipments into the coastal area of Georgia. The law enforcement escort insured that the drug smugglers would be shepherded
through the area's other law enforcement and would, in all probability, get away with their illegal activity. I remember thinking that every
Ranger now would be looked at by the public as a possible suspected smuggler. It's easy to lump every officer into the tainted group
made poison by a few. How would we ever overcome the stain on
the agency's otherwise stainless honor? Every Ranger and trooper
in the state would have to carry the burden of being suspected not
only by the public but also by his or her agency and fellow officers.
Everybody was scrutinized, and no one was exempt.

The commissioner of our department made a courageous and
necessary move and required every law enforcement Ranger to
submit to a polygraph examination by the Georgia Bureau of Investigations. There was, of course, mixed reactions to the news and
quite frankly a few were sweating it. Most, however, looked forward
to the opportunity to clear their good name and return to the nor-
malcy of business as usual. I remember thinking that if the country's
law enforcement officers compromised themselves the nation is in
trouble. I for one jumped at the opportunity to take the polygraph
and clear my good name for the sake of my family, my community,
and my fellow officers. Looking back now, I realize that was the
inspiration to write my paper that year. Ethical and lawful behavior
by members of the law enforcement community should not only be
expected but also demanded by the public. I felt very strongly about
it then and I still do today.

As the day approached when we would go to Tulsa, I became
very anxious. The folks from the Law Enforcement Section that would
be traveling with me were the lieutenant colonel and a corporal from
Waycross who was selected as the State Ranger of the Year that

year. He was to be in another competition and was equally excited to be able to represent his beloved Georgia.

About two days before we were to leave, I began to get a sore throat. I was working a night detail one night and as the hours passed by, it became much harder to swallow. It felt like a serious sore throat and not the usual scratch and tickles. I didn't know it at the time, but I had strep throat and my left tonsil had become badly infected. After a trip to the doctor and a couple of injections, I was ready to travel . . . I thought.

When we arrived at the convention site, we checked into our motel rooms and signed in at the convention table. After we looked around the hotel lobby and talked with Rangers from other states, we decided to go to supper. After supper we went back to the rooms, and I crashed.

The next day I was scheduled to present my paper to the committee and audience. There was about a hundred people in the audience for that session. Each officer was to present his paper and be graded on various categories of the presentation. The paper's content was just a small part of the competition. There was a captain from Texas that presented his paper on electro-fishing that really impressed me. He had about five different electronic fish-shocking devices hidden on his person. I was impressed with his presentation and knew he would be hard to beat. When my time came I went forward with paper in hand and did my level best to represent my department, the state of Georgia, and myself. There was a hearty round of applause when I finished, and it made me feel good to see their response. For just a few moments I forgot about my sore throat and just enjoyed the excitement of the moment.

When they announced me as the competition winner, I almost passed out. I had never won anything like that in my life. I really felt blessed that day. To take top honors at the Southeastern was the greatest honor I could imagine. I couldn't wait to call my wife and tell her the good news. I knew she would be proud of me for sure. The trip home would be much better now.

The drive home was uneventful, and I did a lot of sleeping. I was still not out of the woods by a long shot. When I arrived home, one of the first things I did was to see my doctor again and let him take another look at my throat. More injections!

Oh well, I had made the trip and returned alive and successful. I wondered how many people my paper had influenced. For the next two years or more, I received requests from college students all over the United States and Canada for copies of my paper. I was humbled that a country boy like me had been fortunate enough to be selected for the paper that came from my heart.

- Chapter 24 -
The Snake Show

About the time you think you've seen it all, along comes something that catches you completely off guard. As I was patrolling the county one sunny summer day, I stopped by the shopping center to pick up a couple of items. As I pulled into the parking lot, I could see a trailer parked in the center of the shopping center's large parking area. There was a lot of hubbub going on in its vicinity.

I saw several children with parents in tow as they pulled their moms and dads toward the trailer. My curiosity got the best of me, so I drove my truck over to the trailer to get a better look. To my surprise, there was a sign across the broadside of the trailer announcing, "Snake Show," with a big, colorful, red and green serpent painted along the front of the trailer. It looked like something from a carnival sideshow attraction. People were lined up outside the trailer to pay their 75 cents to see the snakes. It looked harmless enough, and even a bit entertaining. But being a Ranger, I had to check the owner's wildlife exhibition permit and the holding facilities to see if his snake show met the standards set by Georgia law.

As I approached the trailer there was a short, blond fellow taking the money from the people and allowing them to walk inside to get their view of the snakes. I identified myself and asked him if he could produce an exhibition permit for showing the snakes. He looked at me kind of strangely and said, "Permit, what kind of permit?" I told him he had to have an exhibition permit to display the snakes to the public. I asked him if I could see the snakes so I could determine whether they were domestic or exotic. I also wanted to see what kind of pens or aquariums he was using to display the snakes. My main interest at that time was whether there were poisonous snakes that may not be safely stored.

He gladly invited me in so I could take a look. I was surprised at what I found. I couldn't believe the holding tanks these snakes were in. First of all, there were snakes of all kinds from all over the world. There was a green mamba, one of the most deadly snakes in the world. There were two different species of cobra, a boa constrictor, and several snakes that were indigenous to the state. There were rattlesnakes, water moccasins, and nonpoisonous snakes by the dozens like rat snakes, garter snakes, coachwhips, king snakes, and so on.

The trailer was a 35-footer that he had set up as the show trailer. There was a single aisle down the center and holding tanks with glass fronts stacked on either side of the aisle to hold the slithery captives. The tanks were homemade using wood strips and Plexiglas. The display cases were laid out in such a way that the snakes in the lower holding tanks were at face level with the children that would be walking down the aisle. I pushed upward on some of the Plexiglas fronts, and several of them slid upward, exposing the poisonous contents. The way those cases were made, a child could do the same and expose the child's face to the snake. I shuddered to think how dangerous that was.

When I pointed out this danger to the owner, he just admitted that he had not thought about a child pushing up on the front of a case. He also had an old fish aquarium that contained a cottonmouth moccasin that was just about dead from malnutrition. It died later that same day. The whole situation was poorly run and extremely unsafe. I informed the man that he would have to close the snake show until I could contact my supervisors to see what we could do about the situation. This was certainly not your everyday, run-of-the-mill hunting or fishing problem. I had to call the boss on this one. I hung a sign that read "Snake Show Temporarily Closed" at the entrance. The kids were disappointed, but the crowd soon dispersed. Then I placed a call to my supervisor and also to my partner who lived in the county.

My partner arrived first, and we began taking a closer look at the snakes and holding facilities. We saw a military footlocker over in the corner and opened it to see what was inside. Bad mistake! There was a python inside that almost filled up the whole footlocker. Luckily, he didn't move but we sure did. We didn't want that snake loose in the neighborhood.

The captain called us back some time later and advised us to call the Atlanta office and talk to a captain up there to see what he advised us to do about the snake show. We did so and got a call back from him telling us that a herpetologist from the Atlanta Zoo would be coming down to pick up the exotics and that we were ordered to release the indigenous snakes locally.

While we waited for the Atlanta Zoo people, we went ahead and charged the show owner with two violations. One charge was for displaying exotic species without a permit, and the other charge was for failure to provide for the safety and welfare of the animals and the public. Shutting the show down was the best thing for both the snakes and the public.

My partner and I collected all the local species and he carried them to the country to release them. I waited at the trailer for the zoo people from Atlanta. It's a long way from Atlanta to Martinez, Georgia, and it was a long, hot wait in that snake-infested trailer. Finally, just before dark the zoo people showed up and collected the snakes. After giving us a receipt for the snakes, they left. The trailer was turned over to the owner after he posted a cash bond at the sheriff's office. He towed an empty trailer home to Baxley, Georgia, that night.

This ordeal had taken several hours, and I was very tired. I was so tired I had forgotten why I stopped at the shopping center earlier. I was just glad this day was over, but it sure was one to tell my children about when I got home. I had another story to add to my collection.

- Chapter 25-
Price's Bridge

If I were asked for one landmark on Clarks Hill Lake that stood out in my mind as the most meaningful place in my memory, I'd have to say Price's Bridge. Price's Bridge is located on the county line of Columbia and Lincoln Counties on Highway 47 as it passes over the Little River run of the lake. Price's Bridge is near the site of the former Price's Grist Mill that existed before the lake was impounded. I recently had the pleasure of meeting a dear lady who remembered what the area looked like before the lake was impounded. She had lived in the area all her life and remembered it well. She is in her eighties now and remembers every detail of the area as if it was just yesterday. She told me of the old gristmill that was there before the lake was backed up. She also reminisced about how Little River looked before it was turned into a lake. She said there were beautiful white sandbars where people used to come on picnic trips with their families and enjoy the beauty of the river and the millpond made by the grist mill. Of course, all this was much lower than the present lake level.

Today, Price's Bridge is a favorite hotspot of night fishers who tie their boats up under the bridge to fish for crappie, stripers, and hybrids. Boats are tied up side by side under the bridge and stay there most of the night if the fish are biting. Folks hang gasoline lanterns and battery-operated float lights off the side of their boats to attract schools of threadfin shad, which will in turn attract the game fish. On a dark night when the boats are plentiful, it looks like a bright, floating city under the bridge. It's a popular place to fish and therefore a popular place for Rangers to check licenses and boating safety equipment.

During the spring and summer months, especially on weekends, you can check several boats and fishing licenses in a short period of time under Price's Bridge.

It is very precarious work to maneuver your patrol boat in close enough to the boats to check their licenses and safety equipment without hitting their fishing lines. Fishing lines are usually hanging out all around the boats, making it difficult to approach close enough to make your check without disturbing their tackle. When we would approach the bridge at night, we expected that it would take a while to make all the necessary checks.

One of the problems the Rangers are faced with is to know who is fishing and who is not. Some people just come along for the ride and keep their friends company and do no fishing. However, most do fish and one would assume that almost everyone out there was engaged in fishing. The problem is you can't charge someone with fishing without a license unless you can positively testify that you saw him or her fishing. You can imagine how difficult that can be. By the time you come into close enough proximity to the fishers, they can tell that you are the Rangers. Then, all they have to do is lay down their fishing pole and deny they were fishing. We usually approached the bridge from the open water where they could easily see that someone was approaching. In due time, they knew it was the Rangers by the decals and the big blue lights on the boat. We had to let a lot of folks get away with fishing without a license just due to the fact we didn't see them fishing. A guy could just move away from his rod or push it closer to someone who did have a license, until we finished checking and moved on. Then, they would just go back to fishing with the confidence that the Rangers had gone.

One night as my partner and I were headed toward the bridge to check boats and fishermen, we came up with an idea. While we were still a long way out in the open waters, we turned our running lights off and brought the boat to idle speed as we turned and headed toward the riprap that was used to build the roadway. We then tied our boat to a big rock about one hundred and fifty yards from the bridge and climbed up the rocks to the roadway. Then we walked down the road until we got to the bridge. Once on the bridge, we found the bridge pillars, climbed over the bridge railing and perched about 20 feet above the boats below. From there it was easy to look down into the boats and see and hear what was going on. My partner took one end of the bridge and I took the other. We simply lay on the concrete structure on our belly and observed the goings-on in each boat. As we observed, we made notes on who was fishing and who was not. That should put a stop to the "I'm not fishing" routine, because now, we can positively testify that we saw them fishing.

While I was watching a certain boat, I saw a guy take a beer bottle, get down on his knees in his boat and relieved himself into the bottle. Once it was full, he just held it overboard and dropped it into the deep beneath his boat. After filling one bottle, he reached and filled another, until he was finished. I guess when you're out there tied next to other people you can't just stand up and relieve yourself. He was improvising, but technically he was littering. At any rate, I noted this guy and moved on to watch another boat.

After about 10 or 15 minutes of observing from above, we gathered our notes and headed back to our boat. As we walked along the road, we shared stories of what we had seen. Some really funny things happen in the darkness when folks think no one is watching.

When we got back to the patrol boat, we moved at idle speed out into the dark expanse of the open water with our running lights off so as not to be seen or heard. We then approached the bridge from the open waters just as we would have normally done. No one was aware that we had just minutes earlier been above them watching and listening. With this newfound intelligence at our disposal, we began to make our usual checks.

Sure enough, when we came to "Mr. Pee-body," he denied he had been fishing.

"Sir, I saw you fishing that rod a little while ago," I said to him. "Mister, I don't want to call anybody a liar, but I haven't been fishing," he insisted. "Not only have you been fishing," I said confidently, "but a little while ago you relieved yourself into two bottles and sank them overboard." After I said that, he just stared at me. He looked ashen and hollow-eyed in disbelief. He was both amazed and speechless as if he didn't know what to say. His denial ended, and he asked, "How did you know that?" "We have our ways," I said. He was the picture of bewilderment as he pondered the whole thing. While he wondered, I was writing him a citation for fishing without a license. I never told him where we got our information, and I guess he still wonders how we knew. Sometimes, I believe folks think Rangers have a crystal ball or something. We'll just keep them guessing. I suppose you could call this "Operation Skyhook."

There was another night when we were checking boats under the bridge and there were two guys fishing from one of the bridge's pillars. They didn't have a boat, so they had devised a plan to crawl over the bridge railing and climb out onto the top of one of the pillars. Once perched on the bridge pillar, they were just as situated as anyone under the bridge. They just had to hoist their fish further out of the water when they caught one.

As I was checking licenses and safety equipment under the bridge, I looked up to the two guys on the pillar and asked them for their fishing license. The top of the bridge pillars was about 20 feet above the boats, depending on the lake level. It was impossible for me to climb up to where they were from my boat below. They knew that and it seemed to bolster their confidence that I couldn't check them. One of them said in a cocky tone, "If you want to check our licenses, come on up and check them." "You can just hold them up and I can see them from here," I said. "Naw, you come on up and check them," they said half laughingly. The folks in the boats watched to see what I would do next. I just ignored those two and moved down the line checking other boats. I could hear them jeering and laughing but I continued to ignore them. I knew what had to be done.

When I was finished checking the boats, I proceeded to speed away into the darkness of the open waters. I made sure that "Heckle and Jeckle" heard and saw me go away. I wanted them to think they had made a fool out of me and got away without being checked. It is against the law to fail to allow the inspection of a license, so they were getting a ticket if I could catch them. License or not, they were getting a citation for failure to produce a license when requested.

Once I got far enough away, I turned my running lights off and slowly proceeded back toward the riprap just like before. When I got there, I tied my boat up and walked down the road to the bridge. I had made sure I marked which pillar those two laughing hyenas were fishing from.

When I got to the pillar they were on, I climbed over the handrail and onto the pillar with them. You should have seen them. The laughter left them as they realized they were caught. Here they were on the top of a bridge pillar with a game warden and they had no place to go. The only thing they could do was jump into the water and that wasn't an appealing option. "Now, you two jokers show me your licenses," I demanded. "You said for me to come on up here and check them, so here I am, "I said sternly.

The people in the boats below looked up when I pounced onto the pillar, and it was almost like a sigh of relief for them. I think everybody down there wanted these two to be caught. "We ain't got no license," one said. That made my day. Now, they would get two tickets apiece, one for fishing without a license and one for failure to allow inspection.

I guess you could say this was "Operation Skyhook" in reverse. Instead of me observing fishermen from above and catching them below, I had observed these two from below and had gone above to catch them.

To be a successful Ranger you have to be flexible and above all, use your head.

Think out of the box. Do the unexpected. I guess my old days in the Marine Corps had taught me that. Come at them from the least likely direction. It worked for me that night.

- Chapter 26-
The Cock Fight

Cockfighting has been popular in America for so long that it has become, for some, an American institution. The trouble with that is it's illegal. Cockfighting rose to its zenith in the late nineteenth and early twentieth century. At one time there were literally thousands of fans of the so-called sport throughout the United States as well as Central and South America. It is still legal in some countries, but its popularity has been waning in the United States for a long time. Such illegal sports as cockfighting, dogfighting, and bullfighting are illegal in America because of the obvious cruelty to the animals involved.

One winter night in 1979, I was working a night operation with the Ranger in Putnam County. I was assigned to Baldwin County, and we often worked together in one of those counties. Teamwork is better than trying to be a "lone Ranger" and working alone. I preferred working in separate vehicles so we could cover more territory, but the Putnam County Ranger liked for us to sit together. He was a talker and storyteller and his obvious choice was to have someone to talk to.

I had left my truck at his residence and rode with him to the location he wanted to work. We were backed into a hiding place overlooking a big power line right of way that intersected a busy country road. He had been getting some complaints from local folks about someone night deer hunting at that location, so we were trying to catch the culprits. As we sat there in the truck that night, he was telling one story after another and had me in stitches. I enjoyed working with this guy because he was entertaining. His tales had to be made up because they were so unbelievable. Still, he could put a spin on a story that would cause me to laugh so hard that my stomach muscles would hurt the next day.

It was cold that particular night and exceptionally quiet. The traffic on the road we were working was unusually light that night. Then, about 10:00 P.M. we got a call from the sheriff's department in Jasper County. Actually, it was not a call to us specifically. It was a general call to any and all Rangers working in and around Jasper County that night. The only thing the sheriff said on the radio was that he needed all area Rangers to come to the county jail in Monticello. He didn't say why or what the problem was. We knew that for him to ask for outside help was unusual, and he must have needed help right away. We proceeded to Monticello immediately but not in the emergency mode. No blue light or siren was used because the sheriff had said on the radio that it was not a 10-18. That means that it was not an emergency situation on the police radio ten-code system.

As my partner cranked the truck and began to pull out, we discussed what it might be. There was no telling what it was, and the only way we would find out was to go to him. We certainly would help the sheriff with whatever it was. My partner drove there through the back roads and back ways, and we arrived at the jail within minutes after the call.

When we arrived, the sheriff and his five deputies greeted us. Jasper County only had a small sheriff's department back then since it was a rural county. The sheriff didn't fill us in immediately on what was going on because there were more Rangers on the way and he wanted to wait until we were all together before explaining his situation.

Soon, everyone who was coming had arrived and we were all assembled in the sheriff's office for a briefing. In all there were 12 law enforcement officers in the room. There was the sheriff and five deputies from the Jasper County Sheriff's Department and six Rangers. The Rangers who responded to the call were from the counties of Jasper, Putnam, Baldwin, Newton, Monroe, and Butts. I was unaware that there were so many Rangers working that night because we hadn't heard any on the radio. Rangers usually don't talk on the radio unless there is something going on that requires them to break radio silence.

As the sheriff began to explain his situation, he told us that recent intelligence and tips from an informant had revealed that there was a cockfighting establishment out in the county. He said there was a chicken-fighting operation going on at a big barn that was recently built out of old weathered barn lumber. That made it look like an old barn, but it was really a newly constructed building. It looked like an old two-story barn, but it was actually a one-story building. I'll explain that in more detail later. It had been built almost in the yard of the owner of the establishment. The informant said it was in use on that night and that there were about 200 or more people at the location.

The sheriff laid out the plan this way. We would all proceed in a convoy to the location. Upon arrival, the sheriff and the deputies would hit the door of the cockfighting barn and the Rangers would round up everybody in the yard area. The intelligence had revealed that this newly constructed old barn had only one door. That wasn't very smart. The builders had gone to much trouble and expense to make this place, but had failed to account for a police raid. Occupants were trapped inside with only one way out – by way of the sheriff.

When we arrived at the location, it was so exciting. All those law enforcement vehicles sliding in there really stirred up the dust. People in the yard were running as they realized that a raid was in progress. We Rangers all jumped out quickly and began to pick out a runner and give chase. Several were nabbed in the yard and rounded up but some ran into the woods. All the Rangers on this raid were young and in excellent shape. Those guys running into the woods didn't have a chance, although one did manage to get to the creek. He jumped into the creek and submerged himself under the water almost under the embankment. Only his nose and mouth was sticking out of the water as he breathed hard from his run. That's how the Ranger found him. He could hear him breathing hard, and when he shined his flashlight into the creek, he saw this guy with just his nose and mouth sticking out above the surface. The Ranger just reached down and got a handful of hair and pulled him out. They returned to the scene, one drenching wet, and the other grinning.

When things finally quieted down in the yard area, we discovered that the sheriff and deputies were checking identification and taking names. The sheriff advised the people that they were under arrest but being released on their own recognizance. They were being told to come to the sheriff's office the next day and post a cash bond. The reason the sheriff was doing that was because of the size of the crowd we busted. There was no way we could lock all those folks up. The little county jail only had the capacity to hold about a dozen inmates, and we had well over 200 people. As a matter of fact, it was more like 250. I never did get a complete count from the sheriff. We didn't even have a bus to transport them to town if we had to. The sheriff was doing the only thing he could under the circumstances.

After we rounded up the people in the yard, we went to the entrance where the sheriff was positioned to see if we could be of help to him and his deputies. He told us that some people might try to escape out the back of the barn by kicking boards off and crawling out the back way. He asked us to make sure that nobody got out except through the door, which was covered by him and his deputies.

We scattered out around the big building and did indeed find that a board or two had been kicked off the back through which some had escaped. I went around to the back of the structure and found one of the Rangers by the opening created by the missing board. There was a strip about a foot wide and about five feet long down at the bottom where some of them were trying to get away. He was standing by the opening in the darkness so he couldn't be seen from inside the building. He had a firm grip on his metal flashlight, and he was intently keeping the occupants inside. Every time a head would stick out through the hole, he would crack the top of it with that anodized aluminum five-cell flashlight. Ouch! And the head would quickly duck back into the barn. A few minutes later another head would start out and whack! He'd send another would-be escapee back into the barn. He kept this up until they had all filed by the sheriff and his staff to get their medicine.

When I saw that the Rangers had the perimeter of the building pretty well surrounded, I went back to the door to see if I could be of help to the sheriff. My partner and I were there just in case somebody gave the sheriff's deputies a hard time. Not that they couldn't handle it, but we were very outnumbered and any show of force by us could head off any potential trouble.

As I was standing there watching the last few people file out of the building, I saw a tall dark figure of a man come out of the doorway with a cane. He was dressed in black from head to toe and had a beautiful cane with a silver handle. He was moving slowly due to his obvious advanced age. He appeared to be around 75 or 80. As

I looked into his face, I couldn't believe my eyes. He was my daddy's first cousin. I remembered him from my childhood when he would come around to our farm and try to get daddy to raise fighting chickens for him. Raising chickens wasn't illegal and he would offer daddy a good sum of money to handle them for him. Daddy never did oblige him, but his cousin would try nevertheless. He had been in the chicken fighting circles for so long he had gained a reputation and a nickname to match. The gamecock fighters knew him as "Blackie." I had heard that he would even travel to South America to buy fighters. He was really into cockfighting and had been for a very long time.

As he hobbled out of the building and got past the sheriff, I approached him and called him by name. He looked at me with dimmed eyes and squinted to make me out. "Who are you?" he asked. "I'm Jim, Howard's son," I answered. I was in full law enforcement uniform, with gun and badge, and yet he asked, "You with us or you with the law?" "I'm with the law," I said. "Well G__ D___ you," he said abruptly and turned and walked away. That's the last time I ever saw him alive.

After everybody had left that night, we went inside to survey what kind of set-up they had. This cockfighting arena was well lit and had theater seats all around. There were three cockfighting rinks in the center. The middle rink was the biggest and was obviously where the main event was held. The other two rinks were to either side of the main rink and somewhat smaller. That's where the chickens were taken to finish each other off and die. This is a fight to the death sport, if you want to call it a sport. There were dead birds all around and some of the most beautiful tail feathers I'd ever seen. There were also some gamecock spurs that were confiscated that night. These were long, curved, needle-sharp steel instruments that were strapped onto the gamecock's legs to enable him to pierce the opponent to death. Each cock was equipped with these killer spurs. With the deadly instruments attached, they were "pitted" against each other. One of the competitor birds was about to die and maybe both. They were like poultry gladiators, highly trained to kill.

In the top of the building right in the center was a pulley with a rope that ran from the sideline, up to the pulley and down to the center pit. A strongbox was tied to the end of the rope. This was used to place all bets in before the fight and was then hoisted up so everybody could see that the bets were over and no one could tamper with them. There was not much trust among these people. As a matter of fact, my daddy's cousin had spent some time in a prison down in Florida a few years earlier for cutting a man at a chicken fight down there. This was definitely a different class of people.

This wasn't game and fish work but like I've been saying all along, you just never know when you leave home what you are going to get involved with. Law enforcement work is like that. That Jasper County sheriff needed help that night, and you can see who he called on. He called on the Rangers because he knew they would help him get the job done and done right. I hated it that a family member was involved in the bust, but I remember thinking, he chose his lot in life and I chose mine. Our paths crossed and we were on different sides of the fence, but that's life.

- Chapter 27 -
In Conclusion

Other Rangers have written books about their experiences, so this is in no way a claim to originality. Also, I acknowledge that every Ranger has his or her own stories, experiences, and testimonials. I only claim these stories to be my experiences. Every person who puts on the green and gray takes a big step toward an exciting career. It is more than a job. As a matter of fact, it is really more than a career. It is a lifestyle, almost a calling. As a fellow sergeant once said, "It's not everyone who can be a Ranger. Somebody has to flip hamburgers down at the burger-doodle."

If anyone desires to become a Ranger, there are some things they must know beforehand. The advantages are abundant. First, I really enjoyed not having to punch a time clock or having a boss standing over me to make sure I made production. A Ranger has to be self-motivated. He or she must be an energetic person. There is no room for lazy people and those who love sleeping in. There is no boss barking at their heels making them go that extra mile. They have to have such a love for it that they look forward to doing the best they can.

Second, a Ranger's days off and workdays are varied. They have to be flexible because they never know when an emergency will arise that demands their presence. Drownings and hunting accidents don't always happen on scheduled workdays. Sometimes they have to jump into a uniform and respond to emergencies or a violation in progress. If a fellow Ranger needs help, they have to go, and go immediately. They can't drag around trying to find someone else. The off-day schedule is simply a guideline and must be flexible due to demanding circumstances.

Third, the work is varied, which therefore keeps it interesting. Rangers never know from one day to the next what to expect. I have told prospective applicants that you don't know from day to day what you will be doing. You almost never do the same thing every day. That has always been a plus to me because it prevents boredom. You won't be bored as a Ranger. You literally have to be an expert in many fields. Rangers enforce laws that cover activities concerning hunting, fishing, boating, littering, and environmental pollution. Then there is a wide range of peripheral duties that demand their expertise. They have to be an emergency responder, a crowd controller, an expert animal handler, a traffic controller, an expert witness, part scientist, part practitioner, an expert in homeland security, and so much more. When you consider all the things Rangers may be involved in, it is evident that there is no other law-enforcement agency that is so flexible and diverse. There are no law enforcement officers that have to be trained in so many fields, and have such a wide array of authorities, as do Rangers.

Fourth, the hours are varied. There is no shift work in the job of a Ranger. Most other law enforcement agencies work a shift and go home. A Ranger lives in his or her workplace and must respond to the public at any hour of the day. A Ranger may be working early morning one day and late night the next. Or they may work early morning and late night in the same day. On several occasions, I have left home around 4:00 or 5:00 A.M. and did not return home until about the same time the next morning. Since the demands on a Rangers' hours are always changing, they have to manage their own work-hours and make the most of each hour worked. I used to tell young Rangers that they can't hoot with the owls and crow with the roosters on a regular basis. I am reminded of what Sergeant Knox told me about doing my best while I am here and letting the loose ends drag. What he meant was that Rangers can't work 24 hours a day, every day. Sometimes they may work a whole day, and sometimes they may work several days in a row, but they can't work all day every day.

The Fair Labor Standards Act came along and changed the number of hours a Ranger could work in a 28-day work cycle. When I was a Ranger, I worked as many hours I wanted without restrictions. Now, Rangers have to closely manage their time due to the federal law.

Everything I just said about time, days, and duties was told to me the first day of my career. My captain called my wife and me into his office and gave us both a motivational talk about what to expect as a Ranger and a Ranger's wife.

I'm glad he asked her in and gave her this orientation as well as me. It has helped her over the years to understand what to expect from my job and me. Her lifestyle and the lifestyles of our children were affected by my job's demands. It sounds demanding, but I loved every minute of it.

I have said that the only thing constant in state government is change. That is the truth. State government is always in a constant state of flux, and therefore a Ranger has to be flexible and changeable. Laws change, people change, and the agency's leadership changes. I remember that every time we got a new colonel, director, or commissioner, we had to put more emphasis on their projects or particular interests. One colonel may want more waterfowl enforcement, and the next may concentrate on getting the agency certified. Then, another may try to change the administrative structure of the law enforcement section, and so on. Rangers have to be able to change with the flow and adapt and excel. Districts may be changed into regions to save money, which may cost the section more money and time in the long run. But, change takes place and the world goes on.

In all of these changes and demands, the Conservation Ranger marches on doing his or her job while meeting demands and dead-lines. It has been said that the Conservation Ranger is the best-kept secret in state government. They are the work dogs, not the show dogs, of state law enforcement. They quietly get the job done and are not publicity hounds. They are truly a unique agency doing a unique job in a unique environment. It has been said of Rangers (and I quote): "We the willing, led by the unknowing, are doing the impossible for the ungrateful. We have done so much with so little for so long that we are now qualified to do anything with nothing." This little saying was probably born out of the frustration of having to do more with less. There are always going to be budget problems that place more demands on fewer employees. There are obstacles that Rangers seem to overcome year after year. They know how to adapt to change. They are the few, the proud, the Rangers, and I am proud and blessed to have been one of them.

Knox once said, "Jeff, do the best you can while you are here and when you're gone, leave it to some new Ranger." That was good advice. I did my part while I was there and now I've passed the baton on to a new breed of enthusiastic professionals known as the Conservation Rangers.

- Appendix A-
Photos

The author and his partner arrested six persons from the Dublin area for fishing nets illegally on Lake Sinclair. They confiscated 1,200 feet of gill nets and approximately 200 pounds of fish.

Sergeant Jim Hethcox receives a commendation for best paper in the Southeastern presented by Game & Fish Director Leon Kirkland and Colonel Drew Whitaker.

The author receives a commendation from Georgia Governor George Busby.

Author is shown with confiscated female wolf.

Author patrolling the Altamaha River.

A view of the world below.

Looking for turkey bait from the helicopter.

The world
through my
window.

Law enforcement
pilots fly the state
for wildlife offenses.

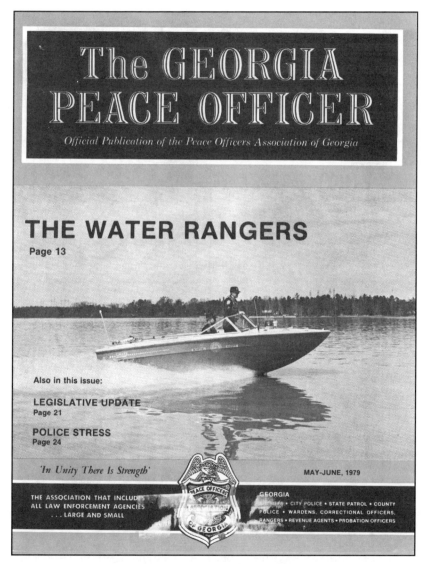

THE WATER RANGERS
Page 13

Also in this issue:

LEGISLATIVE UPDATE
Page 21

POLICE STRESS
Page 24

'In Unity There Is Strength'   MAY-JUNE, 1979

THE ASSOCIATION THAT INCLUDES
ALL LAW ENFORCEMENT AGENCIES
. . . LARGE AND SMALL

GEORGIA
SHERIFFS • CITY POLICE • STATE PATROL • COUNTY
POLICE • WARDENS, CORRECTIONAL OFFICERS,
RANGERS • REVENUE AGENTS • PROBATION OFFICERS

The author and his partner on the cover of the Georgia Peace
Officer Magazine. *Reprinted with permission from POAG and
Callan Publishing Inc.*

Boating safety patrol on Lake Sinclair. *Reprinted with permission from POAG and Callan Publishing Inc.*

The author and his partner checking a fishing license. *Reprinted with permission from POAG and Callan Publishing Inc.*

Corporal Hethcox checks a fire extinguisher while Corporal Nelson checks licenses. *Reprinted with permission from POAG and Callan Publishing Inc.*